Strategies for Positive

Performance in

Government Contracts

Tamara P. Williams, D.B.A.

Author: **Tamara P. Williams, D.B.A.**
Washington, D.C.; drwilliams@aramatandassociates.com

Publisher: **DBC Publishing, Virginia Beach, VA**

Copyright © 2016

ISBN Numbers
ISBN-13: 978-0692771785 (DBC Publishing)
ISBN-10: 0692771786

Connect to the Author

Business Website URL: www.aramatandassociates.com
LinkedIn Profile URL; https://www.linkedin.com/in/tamarapwilliams

TABLE OF CONTENTS

LIST OF TABLES

Strategies for Positive Performance

in Government Contracts

by

Tamara P. Williams, D.B.A.

D.B.A., Walden University, 2016

MA, Webster University, 2013

MS, Troy University, 2005

BS, Central Michigan University, 2001

Doctoral Study Submitted in Partial Fulfillment

of the Requirements for the Degree of

Doctor of Business Administration

Approved by:

Dr. Frederick Nwosu, Committee Chairperson,
Doctor of Business Administration Faculty

Dr. Romuel Nafarrete, Committee Member,
Doctor of Business Administration Faculty

Dr. Lynn Szostek, University Reviewer,
Doctor of Business Administration Faculty

Dr. Eric Riedel, Chief Academic Officer

ACKNOWLEDGEMENTS & DEDICATION

I dedicate this to Carlton Patrick Rollocks and Wilfred Rollocks, two of my biggest supporters. At the time of Carlton's passing in 2005, I was in the beginning stages of my academic journey; the love and encouragement from him as my oldest sibling touched me deeply and has always remained with me. I know in my heart he is still with me and he is cheering me on. My grandfather, Wilfred Rollocks, taught me to read and write at a very young age and incited a passion for lifelong learning. After his passing one month before Carlton (also in 2005), I became committed to continuing the path of education to make him proud. That early education laid the foundation for my academic success today. My family is my life; without their support and encouragement this process could have been more difficult. My grandmother, Lizzie B. Rollocks; parents, Robert and Patricia Williams; brother, Robert P. Williams III; nieces and nephews, Carlton Jr., Nicole, Kimberly, Camille and Aaron, were all instrumental and involved in seeing me through to completion. Their love and support kept me going.

This could not be possible without the guidance and direction of my Higher Power. The people placed in and around my path provided all the tools for completion of this journey. Harry I. Parker, a coworker and a Walden Ph.D. student, introduced me to Walden and suggested I enroll. Without hesitation, I did, and this has turned out to be one of the most inspirational moments of my life. Our near daily conversations about our progress kept me encouraged and never allowed me to think defeat.

The Walden faculty was amazing. My chair, Dr. Frederick Nwosu, was an influential person placed in my path. I had originally requested another faculty member to be my chair. I was assigned to Dr. Nwosu and recognized immediately this was a special connection. His dedication and passion matched my drive to take full advantage of this journey. His timely feedback, constant encouragement, and mentorship was just right for me. I would like to thank Dr. Romuel Nafarrete and Dr. Lynn Szostek for challenging me, as well as fighting for me, and ultimately making this a quality and useful research study. Dr. Freda Turner is an amazing director; she took interest in me when I didn't know she even knew me. The Walden support was like no other educational program I have ever experienced.

I would also like to thank Dr. Carolyn Rose Smith, an amazing resource that helped me get unstuck during the review and IRB processes. The participants of the study were extremely helpful and I would not have had the research data, nor the findings, without them. Lastly, I would like to thank any family I have not already named and friends that were patient when I did not have the time to spend with them. Thanks for all of your support.

Tamara P. Williams

Dr. Tamara P. Williams

ABSTRACT

Past performance ratings of government contractors are becoming a critical pathway to the approximately $300 billion contract dollars the United States Congress sets aside for small businesses annually. This was a descriptive study exploring leadership strategies small business leaders use to attain positive performance ratings in government contracting, viewed through the lens of the principal-agent theory.

The exploration occurred by interviewing 21 small business leaders located within 30 miles of Washington, DC, with favorable performance ratings on at least three government contracting opportunities. Clustering themes according to Moustakas's modified van Kaam helped organize, analyze, interpret, and provide meaning to participant accounts of the phenomenon.

Findings revealed five overall themes: (a) leadership strategies that influence positive performance ratings, (b) behavioral or trait-based attributes of leaders, and (c) understanding bureaucratic dynamics and contract requirements, (d) resource-based capacity as an impediment, and (e) competitive intelligence as a valuable resource. The findings indicated a need for leaders to adapt approaches to contract performance appropriate for the situation as various government agencies implement the requisition and procurement process differently. Identification of strategies that positively influence performance ratings may result in the longevity of small businesses participation or excite those small businesses aspiring or struggling to increase performance.

Findings may also encourage various business leaders within socio-economic groups by providing them tools to actively seek federal opportunities reserved for small businesses, also known as set-asides, along with strategies on how to keep them through positive performance.

CHAPTER I

INTRODUCTION

Foundation of the Study

In the United States, small business participation is critical to continued economic recovery after the Fall of 2008. Effective procurement is an increasingly important subject for businesses providing services to the Federal Government (Dimitri, 2013). Significant contributions defining leadership development strategies have primarily included resources for large corporations. Organizational behavior and leadership characteristics are necessary drivers in small enterprises reaching successful long-term performance in a dynamic and evolving system (Ates & Bititci, 2011). When discussed in the context of performance outcomes, success involves the effective integration and implementation of environmental, social, and financial performance measures (Ameer & Othman, 2012). This research study pertains to measuring small business leaders' performance outcomes in government contracts. The SBA definition of a small business varies by industry and is derived by annual revenue or by number of employees.

To maintain positive performance in any business, organizations' leaders hold an important responsibility in achieving established contract goals. In 2010, the United States federal government made a concerted effort to improve contractor performance by providing feedback to firms through completing Contractor Performance Assessment Reporting System (CPARS) reports (Hiles, 2015). In May 2010, the Office of Federal Procurement Policy designated CPARS as the single government-wide system government agencies now use for entering contractor performance evaluations (U.S. General Accounting Office [GAO], 2014).

The CPARS system is a government-wide system that collects, documents, and houses contractor performance information used by agency decision makers when considering past performance in competitive procurements (GAO, 2014). Developing small business leaders through integrated and disciplined approaches is becoming increasingly important (Mirocha, Bents, LaBrosse, & Rietow, 2013).

Deficiency in research addressing small enterprises and performance initiatives in the federal government has indicated a need for further exploration. Ample effective leadership styles exist for small business practitioners; this study discovered various strategies that leaders of small businesses used that contributed to their positive performance in government contracts. Findings also indicated barriers to positive performance related to attaining subsequent contracting opportunities.

Background of the Problem

Since the Small Business Act of 1953, the central priority for the Small Business Administration (SBA) has been to improve fund flowing to small businesses (SBA, 2014b). As small businesses account for approximately 65% of new United States jobs created, government-contracting dollars have become a vital resource for small enterprises' contribution to the economy (Cronin-Gilmore, 2012). Acknowledging small businesses significance to Americas economy, Congress appropriated approximately $300 billion to small businesses annually (Bublak, 2014). Only 22% of all appropriated dollars equated to contract awards to small businesses, and that deficiency in meeting statutory goals may jeopardize small business' existence (Bail, 2010). Small business owners have been essential to federal government agencies both domestically and internationally (Bublak, 2014). Realizing small businesses pertinence to participation in government contracting predates the SBA.

Despite the SBA's established goals, government contracting resources are still difficult to obtain for small businesses. Since the early 1990s, financial profitability through performance has become a business trend that changed how businesses measure sucess. A need for improvement in government officials ability to assess contractor performance became recognized in the evaluation processes of a contractor's proposed solutions. In 2013, Bradshaw and Su acknowledged the lack of past performance data on both contract performance and companies, contributed to contract program failures, cost overruns, and schedule delays. Fundamental changes in how companies strive to become more effeicient have led to a renewed focus on leadership necessary for creating high-performing organizations (Tideman, Arts, & Zandee, 2013). Leading organizations to perform at high levels has not been enough to produce positive past performance ratings;

therefore, small business leaders have had to change how the organization operates to exceed expectations of key participants in the rating process (Hiles, 2015). As of 2012, the failure rate for organizational change initiatives was 95% (Decker et al., 2012). The emergence of leadership for success has created an information gap germane to leadership and successfully implementing performance measures in organizations (Metcalf & Benn, 2012). Available literature includes small businesses history and role in government contracting; however, current research lack identifying knowledge about strategies available to assist small business leaders' attainment and positive performance in government contracts. Addressing this gap in research served as the focal point for this study.

Problem Statement

Approximately $517 billion, or 25%, of federal discretionary spending goes to contract awards (GAO, 2014; Johnston & Girth, 2012). Incentivizing poor performing contractors cost the government between $15 and $40 billion to fix defective systems aquired from underperforming contractors (Girth, 2014; Shull, 2013).

Data identified 23% of the contract award dollars each year Congress sets aside to incentivize small business participation in government contracting opportunities (Snider, Kidalov, & Rendon, 2013). The general business problem is some small business contractors lack contract business leadership strategies that could increase positive performance in government contracts. The specific problem is some small business contractors lack strategies to achieve positive performance ratings while performing in government contracting.

Purpose Statement

The purpose of this qualitative descriptive research study was to explore strategies small business leaders have used to attain positive, best-practice, performance ratings while performing government contracts. The researcher gained an understanding by interviewing small business leaders located within 30 miles of Washington, DC, with favorable CPARS 'past performance ratings' on at least three government contracting opportunities. Implementing strategies that increase small business performance in government contracting influences social change. Social change may happen through enabling business leaders to create new jobs that increase contributions to the government tax base along with potentially improving the well-being for the unemployed job base this group can employ.

Nature of the Study

The purpose of this qualitative descriptive research study was to explore strategies small business leaders use to attain positive performance in government contracting. The sample population consisted of small business leaders in a 30-mile distance of Washington, DC. Leaders were defined as chief executive officers (CEOs), presidents, owners, or general managers of the organization. A qualitative method with a descriptive design provided the basis for exploration and interpretation into small business leaders' lived experiences. Qualitative research is an inquiry approach useful for exploring and understanding a central phenomenon (Moustakas, 1994; Shields & Rangarjan, 2013). The selected method allows researchers to comprehensively summarize specific events experienced by groups of individuals (Lambert & Lambert, 2012). The data collection technique combined a researcher-created, socio-economic questionnaire and in-depth, face-to-face, semi-structured interviews of small business leaders within 30 miles of Washington, DC. Purposeful sampling was the method used to recruit small business leaders to participate through e-mailed invitations. Researchers use qualitative research methods to describe research informed by explanatory, critical, thorough investigations when attempting to understand multifaceted and complex events (Leko, 2014). A qualitative design provided sufficient information to learn about strategies some small business leaders use for positive performance ratings in government contracting.

Implementing a descriptive design allows data retrieval from members within the desired setting through semi-structured interview questions to understand a phenomenon (Moustakas, 1994; Shields & Rangarjan, 2013). The generic method affords researchers opportunities to advance theories by deviating from methodological prescriptions (Kahlke, 2014). A descriptive design suited this study to explore small business leaders' perceptions about strategies used to attain positive performance ratings in government contracting.

Research Question

The central research question was as follows:

What leadership strategies do small business leaders use to achieve positive performance ratings in government contracts?

Interview Questions

Ten interview questions supported the fundamental research question. The inquiry involved probing the data necessary to explore leadership strategies small business leaders use that facilitate positive performance ratings in government contracts. The 10 interview questions were as follows:

Q1: What leadership strategies do you find most affective for achieving positive performance ratings in government contracts?

Q2: What leadership behaviors do leaders/managers employ that are attributes to positive performance ratings in government contracts?

Q3: How do these attributes influence contract performance ratings?

Q4: How does the contractor-government relationship impede or affect performance ratings?

Q5: What are the impediments or obstacles that small business leaders face when performing in government contracts?

Q6: What resources do business leaders use to assist in achieving positive performance ratings in government contracts?

Q7: What restrictions, if any, discourage small business representatives from achieving positive performance ratings in government contracting opportunities?

Q8: What additional information can you provide to improve leadership effectiveness in small businesses' contracting performance?

Q9: What programs and information will help leaders of small businesses seeking to improve performance ratings in government contracts?

Q10: What programs or information do you suggest to leaders of small businesses seeking to obtain government-contracting opportunities?

Conceptual Framework

Jensen and Meckling's (1976) principal-agent theory served as the conceptual framework for this study. This chapter offers a brief overview with a more detailed explanation provided in the review of the professional and academic literature. The principal-agent theory offers a context for shaping and managing contract interactions to expound the performances amid two actors in agreement (Awortwi, 2012). The principal-agent theory derives from contract law and defines a contractual relationship in which a party engages with another to perform services on its behalf, usually for a fee. When applied to business contracts, the principal-agent theory has broad implications, but the focus is on the respective relational assignments (Steinle, Schiele, & Ernst, 2014).

The principal-agent model includes assumptions. As an economic theory, opportunism is the fundamental concept (Steinle et al., 2014). Relational characteristics create a dynamic where both parties pursue their interest resulting in conflicting goals between the principal and the agent (Fernandez, 2009). If divergent or conflicting goals exist, the principal will respond by monitoring the agent in an attempt to align the agent's behavior with the principal's interest. The presumptuous results encompass a positive contractual relationship cultivating mutual trust developed upon successful goal attainment and responsiveness to principal's interests (Fernandez, 2009). The principal-agent theory provides evidence to explain the relationship behavior between the principals and agents concerning managing contracts (Witesman & Fernandez, 2013). This description thereby served as a plausible framework to assess strategies available for small business leaders to attain positive performance within the contractual relationship context between the two parties.

Definition of Terms

The following are definitions of operational terms used in the study:

Contractor Performance Assessment Reporting System (CPARS): An evaluating tool used for government-wide past performance reporting, mandatory for all government contracts (Federal Acquisition Regulation [FAR], 2014a).

Federal Business Opportunity (FBO): FBO serves as the federal government's primary electronic single point of entry for all open-market contracting opportunities that exceeds $25,000. The FBO website is available at https://www.fbo.gov (FAR, 2014c).

Governmentwide point of entry (GPE): GPE is the single point where the government publically synopsises business opportunities exceeding $25,000. As a public website site, the GPE offers access to any interested companies or individuals (FAR, 2014b).

North American Industry Classification System (NAICS): NAICS codes are size standards the SBA established for small business concerns. The NAICS code describes item categories provided (e.g., supplies vs. services). The codes also qualify small businesses for preferences or eligibility under government programs and procurements (FAR, 2014e).

Set-aside: A set-aside identifies the reservation of acquisitions for the exclusive participation of a particularly identified small business concern. Set-asides occur when an opportunity is open to all small businesses or for a single acquisition or class (e.g., women-owned small business set-aside). They also occur in total or partial set-aside opportunities (FAR, 2014d).

Small business concerns: United States business entities that adhere to SBA-established standard employing fewer than 500 employees and less than $7 million in annual receipts (SBA, 2014c).

Success: Creative thinking strategies crucial to long-term development, successfully directing a company through success related requirements (Newman-Storen, 2014). Success-related requirements include social, legal, political, economic, environmental, ethical practices, employees, and customer concerns (Ameer & Othman, 2012). For this research, performance is used to describe the measure of success. Therefore, in some literature the word *sustainability* is used; however, for the purpose of this study *success* and *performance* were substituted.

System for Award Management (SAM) database: A centralized system the government uses to house certain contracting, grants, and other assistance-related process information for prospective businesses and federal awardee contractors (FAR, 2014b).

Women-owned small business (WOSB) concern: A small business entity where stock ownership by one or more women constitutes 51% company ownership. For consideration in federal acquisitions programs, one or more women must control the daily management and business operations (FAR, 2014b).

Assumptions, Limitations, and Delimitations

Critical scholarly research components, relevant assumptions, limitations, and delimitations for this descriptive study transpired from the epistemologically social constructivist paradigm (e.g., Kahlke, 2014). Considering clearly articulated elements helped set aside biases and inhibited concerns that may have otherwise surfaced and compromised credibility. This section includes situations and circumstances that influenced or impeded methods and data analysis.

Assumptions

Assumptions are essential uncontrollable elements significant to a study. Identified assumptions encompass aspects necessary for the study to exist (Simon, 2011). Assumptions identified presented important features requiring rectifying. This researcher anticipated that participants selected had the experience necessary to answer the central question. Carefully selected individuals and volunteers could withdraw from the study at any time. The researcher assumed participants would answer questions honestly and their opinions and insights would contribute to the research base. Collaborating with industry practitioners, subject matter experts, and participants with extensive experiences ensured credibility (Yang, Kumaraswamy, Pam, & Mahesh, 2010). Selection criteria included purposefully sampled small business leaders who had experience successfully performing on government contracts brought experiences meaningful to the research study's exploration.

Limitations

Limitations are uncontrollable and/or potential events that could affect the methodology and conclusions (Simon, 2011). Limitations included information that was collected and generalized for all contracting opportunities, as well as limited available literature examining leadership and government contracting performance. The interview questions did not permit delineating differences between contract types or government industry classifications. Thus, conclusions are not specifically applicable to all contract types or all services. Service delivery among local United States governments at the state level may differ (Witesman & Fernandez, 2013), which created a possibility findings were constrained from generalizability. The researcher addressed this limitation by collection data at only the federal government level. Government contracting is a broad field ranging from services to manufacturing; therefore, results, as applied to one unique industry contracting with the federal government, may not be generalizable to all industry sectors. Information does not include insight into the applicability among the varying contract types that existed. Finally, limitedly available information on variables that affected performance and government contracts, particularly small business concerns, created limitations for a thorough qualitative discussion regarding published literature within the last five years as of 2016.

Delimitations

Delimitations included controllable characteristics originating from chosen objectives and define anticipated boundaries (Simon, 2011). The study focused on small business leaders located within 30 miles of Washington, DC that were knowledgeable about potential impacts business strategies presented on government contract performance. Regional restrictions are delimitations because findings from participants located within 30 miles of Washington, DC revealed factors that may also affect companies that service government (agencies) throughout the country. Restricting participants to small business leaders means that participants' subordinates could not provide their experience and perceptions of selected participants' management style and performance.

Significance of the Study

Public procurement is a relatively new manifestation to academic research (Flynn & Davis, 2014). *Government contracting* is a common term for United States public procurement from private companies in the commercial sector. Findings served to uncover various strategies employed by small businesses that contributed to positive performance ratings on government contracts. Noteworthy contributions to leadership developments offered insights on how to improve contracting performance. Historically, many findings primarily contributed to large corporations; the resulting effect is a deficiency in information available for practical use by small business leaders (Mirocha et al., 2013). Findings from this study contribute to deficient research for small firms.

Contribution to Business Practice

The information provided by this research study may be useful for small business leaders and government contracting officers in making a decision of finding services using its own human resources assets or acquire services from the commercial sector (3rd party vendor). Implications for practical application of findings resulting from this research study filled gaps in leadership education and provided business leaders and managers with information from industry practitioners desiring to participate in government contracting opportunities. The articulated findings served as contributions to the currently limited empirical literature on leadership strategies and contract performance measurement.

Implications for Social Change

Since 2008, the U.S. economy has relied heavily on employment opportunities offered through small business participation (Cronin-Gilmore, 2012). Discovering potential solutions to business problems surrounding this phenomenon was an additional contribution to limited informational resources on small business performance in government contracting. Identified strategies that contributed to small businesses' participation in government contracts offered more insight into ways to increase performance and contracting opportunities for various classifications encompassed under the broad small enterprises umbrella. Minority-owned, women-owned, and veteran-owned firms comprised of examples where minority government contractor representation may not mirror senior executive representation in federal government agencies (C. R. Smith & Fernandez, 2010). This research helped identify ways to bridge the gaps in representation that may offer opportunities to add value to local economies through employment creation. The results help business owners that fall within the research study's identified socio-economic groups, gain access to federal set-asides and increase their competition for federal government contracts.

CHAPTER II

REVIEW OF LITERATURE

Contracting and Public Procurement

Government contracts, public procurement, and federal contract describe government entities' overarching premise for buying goods and services. These terms include supply chain management aspects under the definition of procurement. Procurement definitions vary in scope in relation to supply chain management, and terms are often industry specific (Miemczyk, Johnsen, & Macquet, 2012). Enhancing supply chain perspectives produces innovative procurement techniques (Gianakis & McCue, 2012). Procurement and sourcing decisions typically concern internal buying processes. The processes relate primarily to direct suppliers (i.e., dyadic relationships) and include specification, vendor selection, contracting, ordering, expediting, and evaluation (Miemczyk et al., 2012). The literature review included a discussion of procurement as a supply chain subsection to understand thoroughly how performance strategies manifest in government contracting.

Contracting involves buying supplies and services from private contractors as an alternative to in-agency services (Awortwi, 2012). Terms used throughout the study are interchangeable expressions used to describe the phenomenon of government procurement. Purchasing as well as supply activities within dyads involve trade-offs or transactions and long-term relationship development with other parties (Miemczyk et al., 2012). Contracting procurement at all levels throughout the federal government is a routine practice (Lu, 2013). Theory and policy indicated competition catalyzed enhanced efficiency in public contracting. Government contracting officials did not always procure supplies and service-based competition or abide by government procurement policy (Joaquin & Greitens, 2012). Decisions to procure supplies or services reflected choices stemming from individual requests or urgent needs, rather than the policies and procedures set forth by the Federal Acquisitions Regulations (FAR). Agency goals and policies, combined with contracting officials' decision to acquire supplies or services, resulted in conflicts. To meet established contracting goals, public procurement officials based decisions on the need to use expedient measures (Snider, Kidalov, & Rendon, 2013). Using convenient measures often promoted non-competitive awards (Johnston & Girth, 2012).

Government procurement and small businesses lacked research regarding successful leadership strategies measured by organizational performance. Understanding strategies small business leaders employ, while considering the contractual relationship between the government and small businesses within the principle-agent framework, was the primary goal of this study.

Organizational perspective. The literature reviewed included public contract performance from various organizational aspects. These elements encompassed universal meaning describing the contractual relationship germane to both the government and the contractor. Apart from regulations that governed the public procurement process, an equally important dynamic was the contracting company's decision-makers who provided input into the contractual relationship (e.g., request for bid (RFB), request for quote (RFQ)) between parties. As a subcategory to procurement, purchasing functions incorporated fundamental public procurement elements in organizations. To account for the different management competencies dimension, business leaders should situate procurement practice on an organizational level as well as a national context (McKevitt et al., 2012). Significant research identified structured purchasing functions and examined how the organization's size influenced purchasing unit designs (and contract acquisition policies) within a company (Glock & Broens, 2013). Provider competition was difficult to achieve, costly to sustain, and contracting decisions may not have included contract management costs (Johnston & Girth, 2012). Insufficient administrative resources for efficient contracting threaten cost-effective outsourcing (Johnston & Girth, 2012).

This section provided additional information and insight into strategies for business leaders that impact government contract performance. Literature derived evidence filled research information gaps on public procurement and contributed to the body of knowledge. Public procurement elements included management competencies, supply management, organizational structure, and information technology (Gardenal, 2013; Gianakis & McCue, 2012; Glock & Broens, 2013;

McKevitt et al., 2012). Other significant elements included administrative resources devoted to managing the market. Resources dedicated to managing the market resulted in pitting market management objectives against contract design, implementation, oversight, and accountability, which entailed actual, often overlooked expenditures (Johnston & Girth, 2012). In public procurement, resources appeared in many forms. In addition to managing contracting markets, other organizational aspects affected public procurement. For example, contract negotiations and final award determinations included factors such as considering the supplier's cost structure throughout the contract cycle (Dimitri, 2013). Additionally, management capacity served as the weak link in determining efficient contracting processes (Joaquin & Greitens, 2012).

Human capital and contracting officers.

Human capital was an essential element to private business organizations' contracting processes with the federal government. Active and normative practices in public procurement highlighted government buyers' management competencies and distinguished procurement professionals according to their skills (McKevitt et al., 2012). Government agency contracting officers were integral in successful make-or-buy decisions to go outside the agency to offer RFB/RFQs for procurement (McKevitt et al., 2012). Government agency leaders settled for provider preference and relied heavily on vigilant monitoring and evaluation activities (Joaquin & Greitens, 2012). A similar conclusion was that agency goals and policies presented conflicting views in the acquisition process requiring alignment to meet established contracting goals (Snider et al., 2013). Even though government decision making officials relied on oversight and monitoring from governmet personnel to ensure contractors met contract deliverables, control of performance became nearly nonexistent at various levels at some agencies (Joaquin & Greitens, 2012).

Studies included a typology of conditions that gave rise to the human elements that could potentially create, enhance, inhibit, and sustain markets from which government procurement officials purchased goods and services. The information revealed theories and governing policies behind public sector contracting needs for products and services. Organizational factors that influenced the contracting process outside the prevailing acquisition policies rendered these principles inapplicability for practical application.

Contracting Goal for U.S. Small Businesses

Small business goals established for each agency
have been the driving force behind small business
participation in government procurement since instituting
the SBA through the Small Business Act of 1953 (SBA,
2014b). Small business goals materialized around the
1940s resulting from deficient contracting opportunities
for small enterprises during World War II (SBA, 2014a).
The lack of opportunities was because the field was not
regulated and agencies could procure goods and
services however they wanted. Applicable government
contracting goals and guiding principles materialized in
1997 in the form of the Federal Acquisitions Regulations.
The FAR established small business goals which aimed
for guaranteed, fair distribution in federal government
contracting opportunities. In 2013, the government set
aside 23% of all procurement dollars to award to small
businesses (GAO, 2014). The federal government had
explicit policies emphasizing promoting small enterprises
through contracting. Complicated programs, goals, set-
asides, and preferences for various distinct groups
amalgamated results (Snider et al., 2013). The push to
adhere to established programs created acquisition

environments centered around convenience measures taken by potentially overworked government procurement personnel (Snider et al., 2013).

Principal-Agent Theory

The principal-agent theory originally derived from contract law and its application to formal contractual agreements has applicability to a variety of management contexts (Witesman & Fernandez, 2013). Supply chain management was an example where theory cultivates appropriate application. Scholars became interested in using principal-agent theory to understand how participants managed risks, aligned incentives, and forged relationships (Fayezi, O'Loughlin, & Zutshi, 2012). Supply chain management had many aspects, and procurement was an essential element in system operation processes (Giunipero, Hooker, & Denslow, 2012; Tate, Ellram, & Dooley, 2012). The principal-agent theory served as an appropriate construct for describing small business leaders' and managers' behavior and performance on government contracts within this research study's context. The theory was a framework for shaping and managing contract interactions to expound performance descriptions for two actors in an agreement (Awortwi, 2012). The principal chooses an agent because the principal lacks the expertise and resources to produce the service in-house and determines if contracting out the services costs is advantageous. Ultimately, the principal hires an agent, and the two parties agree to contract terms including compensation for work performed.

Principal-agent theory in public contracting.
Researchers applied the principal-agent theory to studies involving procurement to describe broad contractual relationship scopes (Awortwi, 2012; Etro & Cella, 2013; Tao & Jingjing, 2011). Studying behavioral choices under incentive contracts involved analyzing monitoring capacity levels to determine value and commission (Tao & Jingjing, 2011). The theory later became useful for examining local governments' effectiveness in managing relationships with private contractors in Ghana (Awortwi, 2012). A competition analysis between research and development firms indicated how market competition relates to incentive contract choices for managers with hidden productivity (Etro & Cella, 2013). Although researchers heavily applied the theory to procurement, public procurement is

a relatively new research topic and a growing phenomenon. How the principal-agent theory has manifested in government contracts, to date, is relatively unknown (Flynn & Davis, 2014). Literature published since 2011 on government contracts management indicated advantages existed to applying the principal-agent theory to government contracting and contractor performance. An example of literature that focused on the application of the principal-agent theory in government contracting involved identifying a gap in research and presenting viable frameworks from which to investigate public procurement studies (Flynn & Davis, 2014). Research scholars have applied the principal-agent theory to government contracting and cited numerous advantages.

Goal alignment. Principal-agent theory elements focused on determining hidden productivity costs and encourage creative ways for principals to measure and compensate agents by minimizing those costs to the principal (Coletta, 2013). The principal-agency theory provides insights for relationship engineering within supply chains, where social, political, legal, and behavioral dynamics dominate (Fayezi et al., 2012). Politics tends to dominate pre-award contract functions;

within this arena, other dynamics affect performance such as goals facing government agencies and federal government contracting businesses. Examining the factors affecting goal alignment, in public sector performance contracts included a focus on Denmark's central government performance contracts. The findings indicated a crucial factor in performance on government contracts is whether agencies control formulating and meeting contractual and agency goals (Binderkrantz, Holm, & Korsager, 2011). Therefore, to improve contracting initiatives, a concentration should be on enabling government leaders to secure realistic and relevant performance objectives from the contractors to the government (Binderkrantz et al., 2011).

Conflicting goals is one of the key problems resulting from the principal-agent relationship. Researchers explored goal alignment through rigorous contract monitoring involving different methods of monitoring performance aspects using surveillance tools such as, establishing performance objectives and performance measures for contracts (Witko, 2011). Performance contracts present a solution to the complexity and ambiguity of required contractual outcomes. The solution was established to allow flexibility in the way tasks could be accomplished.

Performance management examinations combining incentive analysis through performance contracts with executive contracts for agency heads revealed the systems to be ideal for focusing managerial attention on performance (Binderkrantz & Christensen, 2012). The dynamic performance objectives presented the complex contractual relationship from the principal-agent theory perspective. Different national contexts or other public-sector, organization types may reach the same conclusions.

Manage risks and advantages of applied theory. The principal-agent theory has limitations and risks identified by authors researching the topic. For example, an overemphasis on economic drivers has become significant weaknesses in agency theory use (Heracleous & Lan, 2012). The underlying premises of self-interests and conflicting goals, behind the principal-agent theory must remain intact when applying to business and economic contexts, which require broadened conceptions of the two essential elements mentioned (Wiseman et al., 2012). Inductive approaches used to identify context-specific differences between principal-agent and governance structures failed to produce principal-agent relations with applicability to institutional contexts (Wiseman et al., 2012).

Forge relationships and behavior. Applying the principal-agent theory to supply chain management revealed interdependency between the principals and the agents, who often swapped roles within the relationship (Fayezi et al., 2012). In government contracting, the principle is the government agency and any of its representatives (Contracting Officer, Program Official). The agent is the contracting company that has been awarded the government contract and is responsible for delivering services or supplies. Supply chain management theories comprised an appropriate comparison to public procurement research. Closely connected management-specific theories were suitable for use alongside established psychological and economic theories for studying organizations and markets (Flynn & Davis, 2014). Procurement became a supply-chain management subfield. The subcontext was necessary because principal-agency theory elements such as information sharing and incentivization served to explanation relationships and behavior contract alignment (Fayezi et al., 2012). A corresponding principal-agent research model for green supply chain management provided a framework based on the theory

(Kai, Wei, & Meng-lin, 2014). The model was suitable for comparing and analyzing knowledge sharing characteristics between enterprises in green supply chains. The design allowed practitioners to explore features that affected parameters and changed contract formation conditions such as deliverable and contract type. These parameters helped identify and build upon different characteristics established by the analysis and design of a contractual relationship, based on principal-agent theory (Kai et al., 2014). Based on the application of the principal-agent theory in a previous research focused on contractual relationships, we determined the model to be suitable for analyzing this research.

Government procurement officials within government agencies found it difficult to develop long-term relationships with suppliers that would allow optimization in pursuing small business goals established by SBA (Gianakis & McCue, 2012). Relational contracting or informal, unwritten agreements relied upon a structured agreement, which means the relationship was more than between just two parties (Never & de Leon, 2014). Because there are no written agreements in this type of contracting, terms can be easily changed and all performers, prime and subs are subject to changes. Government contracting is governed by the FAR. Relational contracting is how government contractors market to the government, however, at some point these agreements become formal. A formal process follows policies and procedures that promote fairness and best value. Never and de Leon (2014) found that trust was crucial to ensuring all individuals sought mutually beneficial solutions so the relationship would continue. While the literature indicated difficulties in forming relationships, the findings also indicated the importance of relational contracting for successful contractual performance and completion.

Rival theories and opponents of the principal-agent theory. Numerous theories stood out for their predominant use in public procurement research. Two were most prominent: the theory of auctions and competitive bidding and principal-agency theory (Flynn & Davis, 2014). Based on historical United States contracting regimes, relational contracting and the stewardship model typified classical contract law (Van Slyke, 2007). The theories addressed significant discussion underlining contractual relationships highlighting the similarities shared. For example, primary factors underlining the principal steward relationship included goal congruence, mutual trust, and benefit

(Witko, 2011). Within the principal-agent theory, researchers revealed managers frequently contacted and communicated with their vendors despite having clear structured and formally written contracts, which resemblances attributes of relational contracting and the stewardship model (Lamothe & Lamothe, 2012b). The contact alluded to prospects that actual contractual relationships deviated from the theory the agent acts out of self-interest to relationships where managers and contractors maintain trust and partnership.

Formal written agreements such as those drafted within the principal-agent theory context contained influencing factors such as service characteristics, market conditions, and vendor ownership (Lamothe & Lamothe, 2012b). These factors differed from more relational agreements that contained influence from management style such as reputation, management capacity, and continuing relationship expectations (Lamothe & Lamothe, 2012b). When discussing success of government contractors, the factors and activities allowed by the principal-agent theory relationship may not permit flexibility in communications between the principal and agent. Limitations characteristically exist that are historically requisite for maintaining such a contractual relationship.

Relevant work from the contractor perspective came from authors who explored public contracting for human services based on the impact on the contractor rather than the government (Never & de Leon, 2014). A focus on relational contracting by Never and de Leon (2014) involved viewing the event from the trust theoretical framework. Viewing the relationship expanded Van Slyke's (2007) instrumental work in examining relationships between government agencies and contractors and contended that relationships between public bodies and entrepreneurs often more closely resemble principal-steward relationships. The descriptive findings indicated government agencies were unreliable to human service, non-profit companies that prevented the non-profits to adhere to predetermined contractual responsibilities (Never & de Leon, 2014). The contractor to the federal agency bore the burden to reduce their financial or human capital (Never & de Leon, 2014). Goal alignment for any service and establishing rapport became important factors for satisfactory performance within the contract requirements and Statement of Work (SOW). The government's standing on performance measurement and approval of the work performed under the contract, was a significant factor dictating the contractor's approach to leading and managing their organization in providing the services or goods to adjust performance to please the principal (the federal government agency and contracting officer).

Measures of Performance

Past performance as it relates to government contracting is an evaluation factor comprised of work experience, relevant experience, and how well the company performed the contract SOW (Hiles & Wells, 2015). Researchers argued favoring a positive relationship between success and financial performance, because success efforts improved economic benefits by enhancing relevant organizational aspects of both parties (Lee & Pati, 2012). Information derived from the literature analysis indicated a deficiency in universally accepted performance standards or methodologies for measuring, assessing, and monitoring the company's progress toward successful performance. Government personnel may be tempted to subjectively evaluate performance based on the relationship formed, not necessarily based on performance or contractual outcomes. Corporate interest in successful performance resulted from poor past performance including environmental disasters, social scandals, previously lax government regulations, and increasing consumer concern for ecological-based, environmental issues (Makipere & Yip, 2008). An analysis by H. Walker, Miemczyk, Johnsen, and Spencer (2012) substantiated research findings and identified, measureable performance related to social (or societal), ecological, and economic dynamics as primary successful procurement and supply chain aspects.

The research study's literature review on success indicated inconsistencies in successful performance, as outcome measurements surfaced from varying perspectives. One investigation to identify strategies related to corporate performance included organizations whose leaders reported corporate success practices to examine their impact on financial performance (Ameer & Othman, 2012). Sampling 100 top global corporations confirmed companies whose leaders place emphasis on success practices had higher economic performance (Ameer & Othman, 2012). Economic performance as measured by return on assets, profit before taxation, and cash flow from operations was comparable to companies without such commitments in some activity sectors (Ameer & Othman, 2012). Another approach to examining successful corporate performance from an economic performance perspective showed limited focus on the service industry (Lee & Pati, 2012). Using the Pacific Sustainability Index to sample 196 companies from 12 industries ultimately exposed a direct relationship between the environmental, social sustainability factors and market performance. A multi-industry, empirical study centralized to purchasing managers identified trends, methodological challenges, and research gaps from sampled articles published in the *Journal of Purchasing and Supply Management* (H. Walker et al., 2012).

Engaging in processes of transforming corporate leaders to enhance contributions to larger successful development delivered sucessful value beyond financial growth (Kiron et al., 2013; Tideman et al., 2013). In some industries, Leadership in Energy and Environmental Design (LEED) certification programs facilitated this process. One empirical test assessed factors that influenced U.S. companies decisions on adopting LEED certification programs (Gauthier & Wooldridge, 2012). Publicly available information provided support for the argument that imagination drives LEED adoption among organizations (Gauthier & Wooldridge, 2012). The data collected contributed to investigative literature that determined successful innovation adoption (Gauthier & Wooldridge, 2012). No matter how organizational leaders approached successful growth, the research showed high potential for implementing successful programs. Many company leaders proceeded with incorporating success initiatives because resources and capabilities resided internally; however, the ability to add value depended upon supporting routines (Perego & Kolk, 2012). Unconventional methods were organizational leaders' responsibility to determine the best course forward to achieve successful progress for a company's future.

Successful Procurement Performance

Successful procurement appeared most frequently defined as the pursuit of successful business development objectives through the purchasing and supply chain process (H. Walker et al., 2012). The most common definition was applicable, as no universal definition of success or successful procurement performance existed. Successful procurement is a growing phenomenon as there have been an increasing number of special issues on successful operations management, and successful purchasing and supply since 2012 (H. Walker et al., 2012). Concepts used to explain successful supply chain management were applied to explore strategies facilitating positive performance in government contracting (Giunipero et al., 2012). The traditional primary focus of successful procurement was reducing costs to the government (Giunipero et al., 2012). Government initiatives to improve contract completion goals included avoiding cost overruns through government contract management via contractor performance. The exploration of small business contractor evaluations of performance included minimizing cost overruns through leadership efforts.

In studies, researchers explored performance objectives that included prices supporting the success of upstream supply chains (Ageron, Gunasekaran, & Spalanzani, 2012). The theoretical framework developed for successful supply management focused on contractor suppliers and their firms' involvement in formulating and managing a successful business. Management initiatives and government regulations primarily dictated purchasing and supply chain success efforts (Giunipero et al., 2012). A hindrance to performance initiatives for many companies included lack of strateigic financial investments during economic uncertainty (Giunipero et al., 2012).

Success for organizations included critical areas that collectively created a systemic, strategic focus that helped foster successful growth for business stakeholders and federal government agencies. It was unclear if business leaders pursued success measures to benefit the contractor business. Upon initial implementation, external pressure from government regulations and consumer perceptions toward environmental responsibility compelled organizations to pursue environmental activities (Tate et al., 2012). Business Executives acknowledged their naivete of clear definitions of success initiatives by reporting a lack of consistency in selecting and implementing successful performance activities in areas such as supplier and buyer investments at the Chief Executive Officer (CEO) level (Giunipero et al., 2012). Around 2004, academic researchers began to contribute to the literature on supply management strategies to enhance performance from perspectives that did not focus on reducing cost, to devise methods for measuring successful leadership (Lourenço, Callen, Branco, & Curto, 2014). Based on performance outcomes from the research findings, successful leadership was found to have involved the interaction between environmental, social, and financial performances (Ameer & Othman, 2012). Senior leaders in commercial businesses tended to capture success policy and practices by adopting dedicated language and financial auditing processes (Perego & Kolk, 2012). That policy and practice ensured they met commercial and professional objectives through internal audit reporting (Boiral & Gendron, 2011). The reporting alluded to a trend that organizational leaders would incorporate and embellished reports of successful progress for financial gain or to retain stakeholders' trust.

Leadership Performance

Leadership is a subject that includes many topics, and theories continue to emerge as leaders face circumstances dissected by researchers seeking to stay abreast with changes in business practitioners' experience. Common themes from the literature reviewed explained perceptions of business leaders incorporating strategies facilitating positive performance ratings on government contracting opportunities, which were applicable to principle-agent theory characteristics. The themes commonly applied to the principle-agent theory signified the ability of leadership and manifestation of positive performance within that framework. Ultimately, leadership was inclusive and emergent, and promoted initiatives for growth and stability.

Findings from literature published within the last five years (pre-2016) enhanced transformational leadership research through a sustainable leadership theory (Tideman et al., 2013). Authors suggested measuring successful performance by the creation of long-term value of the organization by embracing opportunities and managing risks stemming from economic, environmental, and social issues (Makipere & Yip, 2008). Leadership and organizatoinal performance is broad in scope. Collectively the two concepts reveal the disruptive and transformational changes that occurred in business and society, given the modern complexity context and stakeholder interdependence requirements (Tideman et al., 2013). Leadership theories researched from an organizational performance perspective indicated a dependence on collective goals and objectives like maximum profit, good quality product, increased share in the market, profitable financial results and an effective strategy for development (Khan & Adnan, 2014). Using available resources have been recognized as effective strategies for achieving those leadership goals and objectives (Khan & Adnan, 2014).

Performance and leadership continued to evolve as important business essentials to achieve human, physical, financial, and information goals and objectives by an organization. Questions from scholars remained about strategies small business leaders used when leading their organization and what constituted a good leader in business. Since 2011, research findings indicated ethical behaviors such as integrity in operations and reporting, and leadership tools helped organizational leaders improve performance and respond to consistent global and economic changes (McCann & Sweet, 2014). A leader for successful organizational performance should be able to transition from a culture of power and control to a cultre of exhibiting open-mindedness, moral courage, and a high degree of self-knowledge (Tideman et al., 2013). The changes in leadership perceptions evolved from a mindset that past successes to business challenges were not good indicators of future success because leadership challenges may differ entirely (Tideman et al., 2013). Findings in Tideman et al. (2013) were similar to those rendered by McCann and Sweet (2014), and both indicated a required shift in leadership knowledge, culture, and skills to solve future problems within the organization.

Leadership behavior for successful

performance. Behavioral theories assisted in describing the behaviors business leaders used to interact with others, including followers. Within the influencing environmental sustainability context, leaders high in intellectual stimulation encouraged subordinates to think about environmental issues (Robertson & Barling, 2013). Leaders addressed environmental sustainability through encouraging subordinates to question long-held assumptions about their own and their organization's environmental practices and address environmental problems in an innovative manner (Robertson & Barling, 2013). The interaction required to facilitate successful change through leadership included establishing durable personal relationships both inside and outside the organization by working collaboratively with others (Mittal & Dorfman, 2012). When discussing organizational behavior impacts, Robertson and Barling (2013) focused on how leaders and leadership behavior affected the workplace and the ability to foster employees' behavior to pro-environmental change. The information was necessary because it replicated and expanded knowledge derived from transformational leadership studies and provided a link between transformational leadership and leadership for success.

When explored through the strategic leadership and neo-institutional theoretical frameworks, Strand (2014) classified a small group of individuals who occupied leadership or executive positions within their organizations with the power to facilitate successful change in business practices. When exploring ways in which responsible leadership influenced organizational processes and outcomes, Doh and Quigley (2014) linked responsible leadership by explicating the pathways through which responsible leaders influence outcomes at multiple levels within organizations. The linkage led to descriptions of two pathways through which leaders and their organizations exhibited responsible leadership behaviors and action (Doh & Quigley, 2014). The two pathways occurred through knowledge sharing and dissemination, or psychological enrichment, or a combination of both.

The results from surveyed CEOs and senior executives at companies participating in the UN Global Compact meetings indicated leadership behaviors for successful performance employed a long-term view and advocation for continuity (Tideman et al., 2013). The survey also revealed that while exhibiting open-mindedness, moral courage, and extraordinary self-knowledge, these behaviors flowed through the mindset centered in consciousness and continuity (Tideman et al., 2013). Business leaders could instill this position pro-actively to realize external opportunities that may have otherwise gone unrealized without incorporating the strategic level position (Robertson & Barling, 2013). Leaders who exhibit individualized consideration displayed compassion and empathy for employees' well-being and help employees develop their potentials and skills (Tideman et al., 2013). Comparing successful business factors and leadership theories revealed leaders must fundamentally change the way they think, that is, their mindset or consciousness (Tideman et al., 2013). In doing so, leaders established close relationships with followers, in which they could mentor and transfer environmental values, model environmental behaviors, and raise questions about environmental assumptions and priorities.

Leadership styles for successful performance. Examining existing leadership styles revealed two prominent leadership styles supporting relevant traits for successfully implementing corporate social responsibility and successful performances in organizations (Metcalf &

Benn, 2013). The leadership styles discussed maintained similarities in associated behaviors and how they affected the organization's human complex system. Traits and outcomes emphasized prominent leadership styles associated with success collectively supported fiscal performance within a company. For example, transformational, complexity, and emergent style leadership were suitable because the behaviors varied and offered the most appropriate platforms for exploring new ideas (Metcalf & Benn, 2013). Servant leadership is similar to transformational leadership in success and organizational performance research. Transformational, servant, and spiritual leadership theories contained behaviors and outcomes consistent with the framework for leading the transformation to performance excellence (Latham, 2013a, 2013b). Perceptions of transformational leadership and servant leadership styles had a high correlation. Principal servant leadership perceptions included empowerment foster satisfaction, commitment, and intention to stay in volunteer service organizations (Schneider & George, 2011). The authors noted above provided information critical to success in leadership research as the information provided viewed the phenomenon through the complex systems theory to measure leadership effectiveness within complex adaptive organization systems. Both leadership theories correlate to long-term success, performance outcomes (Graves, Sarkis, & Zhu, 2013), and value for multiple stakeholders (Latham, 2014). This literature review emphasized transformational and servant leadership theories in successful business performance.

From a government perspective, Strand (2014) described success implementation as intricate processes promoting concrete environmental, economic, and social concerns. Leaders and leadership are elements that make or break the organizations adaptivity to complex systems that interact with it (Metcalf & Benn, 2012). The focus of Metcalf's study was on highlighting leadership styles and behaviors for complex organizational systems and processes that affected performance within the principal-agent theory framework to influence performance.

Transformational leadership. Through transformational leadership, leaders used their relationship with subordinates to control them intentionally and encourage them to engage in workplace pro-environmental behaviors (Robertson & Barling, 2013). Transformational leadership had ties to leadership for successful performance through a link to innovation this leadership style encouraged (Metcalf & Benn, 2013). This facilitated exploring the theory that transformational leaders communicated clear and coherent environmental visions under their responsibility. In leading for success, leaders led by sharing their environmental values with employees to demonstrate commitment to addressing environmental problems (Graves et al., 2013). The results provided support to the conclusion that positively related environmental transformational leadership improved employees' motivation to perform (Graves et al., 2013). Graves et al. (2013) findings consistently linked success and leadership elements to performance. The analysis and subsequent connection provided insight into performance achievements, which related to the purpose of this study.

Studies that explored leadership for successful performance through the transformational leadership theoretical lens emerged with a common finding: pro environmental behaviors (Robertson & Barling, 2013). When evaluating leadership from a successful corporate brand, the results were consistent. The guiding principles behind the successful corporate brand leadership concept included personal values such as fairness, trustworthiness, and concern for the environment and communities (Stuart, 2013). When analyzing all elements previously discussed, the themes that emerged were consistent whether addressing environmental, economic, or social concerns.

Servant leadership and successful performance.

Servant leadership is a phenomenon in which leaders establish follower growth as the top priority (Schneider & George, 2011). A link existed between considering stakeholder needs and psychological benefits to members through the leaders commitment to creating value for the community (Doh & Quigley, 2014). Servant-leadership played a role in success, as it had close ties with transformational leadership with overlapping characteristics between the two theories (Latham, 2014).

In an organization, a servant leader served his or her employees, customers, and community to help people develop, strive, and flourish (Gupta, 2013). The servant-leadership philosophy, which emphasized leading in a successful manner, was most appropriate for measuring performance from a successful approach as opposed to short-term economic gain (Gupta, 2013). From a normative perspective, servant-leadership required leaders to recognize their moral duty constructively to improve the larger communities in which they operate (Mittal & Dorfman, 2012). From a social business perspective, Gupta (2013) explored servant-leadership in success. The underlying objective was also the same criterion by which performance evaluation played a part, which was to create social benefits. Social benefits aligned with performance in government contracting, where contractor performance benefited both the principal and the agent. Organizations' leaders that supported the public sector, by performing services for them, limited focus on growing followers, increased efforts to creating value, and preserved the principal's interest. The focused responsibility in relationships and people took priority over the tasks. Servant leadership had many behaviors that aligned with success concepts; however, critics contended that behaviors neglected concern for products. The results included neglected product output, goal setting, and vision creation (Gupta, 2013). Although researchers noted possible downsides to servant leadership, there has yet to be a consensus among them. The reasons stemmed from varied traits and behaviors and a lack of unanimity regarding a theoretical framework for researching.

The literature analysis on success in leadership

revealed deficient documentation within the principal-agent theory framework. The uniformity in premises among researchers was that performance and success in leadership did not have precise definitions. The review involved an attempt to clarify success in leadership through characteristics and definitions from varying perspectives and leadership styles to find common attributes.

Small business leadership. Leadership is an important responsibility in an organization. When discussing small business in leadership, especially in public contracting, it was important to consider the size and classification. Federal statistical agencies use North American Industry Classification System (NAICS) to collect, analyze, and publish statistical data related to the U.S. business economy (US Census, 2016). In public sector contracting, small business is an entity that employs less than 500 employees and averages less than $7 million in annual receipts (SBA, 2014c).

Leadership in small enterprises is a heavily studied topic. The increasing information on the subject indicated different leadership behavior views within organizations that vary with the situation or circumstance encountered (Psychogios & Garev, 2012). The infused theories indicated for leadership styles to correlate with positive organizational performance, leaders might have had to adopt a hybrid leading style. The sophisticated leadership styles nurtured organizational effectiveness. Loose organic structures, employee empowerment, and self-organization materialized as the most prevalent behaviors that enhanced business effectiveness (Psychogios & Garev, 2012). Complex business systems, with rapid changes in technology, population, economic activity, and the global dealings, existed in multiple environments. Relating complex systems proved useful as they almost mirrored the environmental uncertainties that contractor companies (agents) entered when adapting to federal government agency (principal) needs.

A study on small businesses leaders' traits and skills in Lebanon revealed a commitment to attaining excellence was a significant factor in their success (Fahed-Sreih & Morin-Delerm, 2012). In Bangladesh, small businesses used primary employment avenues and achieving organizational goals was critical (Kayemuddin, 2012).

While researchers focused on participants from different countries, the research study findings may have generalizability as leadership is a universal theory. The potential for various findings in previous studies included culture, participants, evaluation method, and sampling size (Fahed-Sreih & Morin-Delerm, 2012). A multiple regression analysis sampling of 206 small businesses conducted by Yan and Yan (2013) involved investigating the relationship between leadership, organizational citizenship behavior, and innovation in small firms. Some organizational citizenship behavior elements had a significant and positive relationship with change (Yan & Yan, 2013).

When discussing successful performance related to leadership, Avery and Bergsteiner (2011) concluded that companies whose leaders placed an emphasis on success, which included leadership factors as an essential element, flourished in various countries. When compared to the shareholder first approach, extensive evidence existed to show that successful practices were the likely indicator to enhancing business performance (Avery & Bergsteiner, 2011). Diversity in leadership, and including minorities in senior executive positions, resulted in a greater percentage of small businesses receiving federal contracting opportunities (Fernandez et al., 2013). Successful leadership features adhered to impart worldviews, mindsets, beliefs, and attitudes embodied by both leaders and followers (Tideman et al.,

2013). These elements became important progressions of relevant skills to facilitate leadership transformation for successful development. In some organizations, bureaucratic structures, and key performance indicators drove corporate performance initiatives (Strand, 2014). Successful performance was contingent upon more than just leaders' ability to implement effective strategies and includes small business leaders' ability to maneuver bureaucratic environments in which the manager operated. Problems arose for small business leaders supply networks attempting to modify or even maintain structure by implementing a successful procurement strategy.

Women in small business leadership.

Women's representation increased in the corporate office in Fortune 500 firms from 8.7 to 15.7 percent since 1996, and academic scholars had taken an interest in how female business leadership affected business outcomes (Matsa & Miller, 2011). Gender and ethnic concerns incorporated stereotypes, group interactions, role expectations, and power differentials into leadership style and organizational culture. In 2013, the government sought to conduct increased contract procurement and acquisition business with women-owned firms and set aside 5% of total prime and sub-contract dollars for women-owned small businesses (Snider et al., 2013). In women-owned business entities, the combined women management, as well as ownership must amount to at least 51% (Matsa & Miller, 2011). The social and ethnic values women held entailed documented differences in corporate directors' preferences and values (Adams & Funk, 2012). Trends indicated a need to encourage the inclusion of women. For example, women-owned firm's leaders downsized their workforce less than their male counterparts did during December 2007 and June 2009 (Matsa & Miller, 2011). Women in business and leadership contributed to business, yet historically women were substantially under-represented in corporate leadership (Mcdonald & Westphal, 2013). As the exploration of women in leadership continues to develop, recognizing the impact on leadership styles, the need to include different skill sets in leadership, and embracing socio-economic groups may yet materialize. In an attempt to explain gender differences in owners, non-contributing factors included age, education, or net worth (Matsa & Miller, 2011). Women leaders had greater concern for their workers well-being, often sacrificing short-term profits. Women owners willingness to compromise suggested a difference in the manner or style in which women led as being the difference in their success. Company leaders recognized including women and minorities in leadership positions as essential practices. Gender and culture in leadership represented important topics, because these values helped mold individuals' identities and, therefore, affected the choices made and how they led.

Performance Measurement and Outcomes in Public Contracting

Government officials maintain past performance reports as a determining factors in vendor responsibility. Although compliance levels with reporting requirements had improved by 18% since 2011, the compliance rates with reporting varied from 13-83% by organization (GAO, 2014). The principal-agent theory has a framework for monitoring various contract outcomes, which included performance measurements. The concepts and methods, as mentioned previously in supply chain management and public procurement, retained transferability and applicability. A greater goal alignment between public and non-profit organizations meant that non-profit organizations leaders could demonstrate higher reliability in performing work for government entities, thereby resulting in a higher effectiveness level (Awortwi, 2012). Substantial factors discussed involving vendor performance impacts entangled the government's close cooperation with its contractors, in addition to political connections (Lamothe & Lamothe, 2012a). The untraditional relationship between the government-agency, deciding-official and the business contractor aligned with Awortwi's (2012), who concluded the most significantly perceived contractual performance indicators are contractor selection and contract monitoring.

Considering reflected activities and behaviors presented in the principal-agent relationship, universal, non-discriminant performance measures existed (Witesman & Fernandez, 2013). An e-procurement model for public contracting authorities to quantify procurement performance benefits assisted the industry by measuring how e-procurement contributed to increasing organizational performance (Gardenal, 2013). Goal alignment was an important factor in measuring and predicting successful government contractor performance irrespective of the size, type of company, or the contract type. Contracting performance was a by-product resulting from trade-offs existing between different aspects such as costs, delivery schedule, technology enhancements and risk contained within the contracting relationship (Awortwi, 2012). In exploring contracting effectiveness and government's performance, performance management included a focus on correlations between various factors the authors selected to investigate (Chaturvedi & Gautam, 2013). The documented processes rendered positive impacts on several key, high-performing organizations' indicators (Chaturvedi & Gautam, 2013). The findings showed the initiative to record contractor performance during and after contract delivery, had the potential to contribute toward civil servants' performance orientation. The efforts also helped government agency leaders push for reforms and good governance such as instituting a government wide contractor performance rating system and instituting mandatory training for reporting officials.

When discussing performance measuring from the government perspective, the rating official almost invariably relates to principal-agent theory concepts. Since 2011, studies included discussions on performance within the principal-agent theory context (Awortwi, 2012). Some research addressed performance specifically as it related to government contracting (Chaturvedi & Gautam, 2013), while other reseachers incorporated dynamics such as political connection impacts on vendor performance (Lamothe & Lamothe, 2012a). In the study named above, researchers reviewed independently contributed to the body of knowledge in some form. When addressing elements focused on answering the central research question, authors failed to specifically address strategies for leaders of government contractor organizations to attain positive performance ratings within the principal-agent theory framework.

Contract Performance Leadership Ramifications

Poor performance ramifications were and are still detrimental to small business participants, but especially in the government contracting industry. When contract performance suffered, performance or contractual agreement breaches occured (Jacobi & Weiss, 2013). In assessing default remedies for contract breaches, economic determination motivated renegotiating the contract, or seeking default remedies by the federal contracting officer (Jacobi & Weiss, 2013). Among the remedies for breaches in performance are the collection of present and future payments (Jacobi & Weiss, 2013).

Performance rating implications. Positive performance ratings and contractor performance systems were critical for continued opportunities for business and contracting entrepreneurs, as government contracting officers sought experienced and qualified business partners to achieve procurement objectives (Bradshaw & Su, 2013). Creating performance measures had positive implications on the federal decision-makers' capacity to manage contracts successfully (Amirkhanyan, 2011). These factors made positive performance an imperative goal for government contractors; standardized requirements for increased accountability by performance measurement resulted in decreased risk of contractual deficiencies (Amirkhanyan, 2011). Multiple GAO findings showed the government reporting system and processes for analyzing and reporting performance lacked the capacity to provide effective results (Amirkhanyan, 2011; Bradshaw & Chang, 2013). Regardless of accuracy of data internal to federal officials, the performance reports helped government officials determine whether a contractor received, or would be eligible to receive, future work (Bradshaw & Chang, 2013). Notwithstanding the deficiency in performance reporting, performance reporting is public information once published. The records viewable by any interested party. A negative impact on poor performance ratings potentially extended beyond the lost revenue from future potential contracting opportunities, but could jeopardize the existence of small businesses relying solely on revenue from government contracts. As discussed previously, procurement officials considered past performance reviews in source selection processes. Contractors must focus on relationship building and contract deliverables to establish a record of positive past performance in this arena.

Adversarial relationships. Building coalitions with the principal company facilitated positive attributes to successful performance aligned with the principal-agent theory theoretical framework. Success in procurement supply chain processes included creating value for multiple stakeholders and the principal (Latham, 2014). Communication and organizational structure predominantly influenced mutual relationships that relied heavily on perception (Grudinschi, Sintonen, & Hallikas, 2014). Collaboration and partnerships were essential to public service procurement (Grudinschi et al., 2014). Both variables, communication and collaboration, substantiated and extended the research conducted by Plane and Green (2012), who concluded value for both buyers and suppliers emerges when maintaining a successful collaborative relationship.

While literature existed that helped emphasize the connection between the government and contractors; adverse relationship implications disputes in performance objectives were unclear and undefined. Contradictory procurement approaches did not necessarily preclude collaborative relationship maturation (Plane & Green, 2012). Striving to create such a relationship may prove more valuable to both parties.

Contractual ramifications. Since 2012, suspension or debarment is a process and tool for the government to avoid doing business with non-responsible contractors (General Services Administration [GSA], 2016). The ramifications for poor performance are critical and possibly detrimental to business leaders and the companies who lost the contracts. Potential negative contract consequences included suspension or debarments, which were and still are serious matters. Creating and implementing comprehensive values-based ethics and contract compliance programs, as recommended, was and still is the best way for government contractors to avoid potential suspensions and/or debarment (Lasky, 2013). Other statutory powers available to the government for implementation against underperforming contractors included terminations. Terminations for convenience under a traditional fixed-price contract allowed the government to breach contract terms legally when it benefits the government (Korman, 2014). Terminations are not routine, but happen when the Government either loses funding or no longer requires the services under contract. The enactment of termination clauses authorized by the FAR subsequently entitled the contractor copmany to recover costs such as post-termination settlement costs, and lost anticipated profit for the remaining terminated contract (Korman, 2014). Terminations for default became enforceable when a contractor defaulted on contractual agreements. In terminations for default, the contractor became liable for assessed claims for replacement products, price increases, and administrative costs (GAO, 1994). The financial repercussions to terminations usually meant the difference between small business growth or death.

Summary

This research study's literature review revealed studies conducted in government contracting and small business left a gap in research on strategies for small business leaders and their role in achieving positive performance in government contracting. Previous researchers omitted information on leadership styles and government contractor performance in their studies. More opportunities for research with an expansive scope exists for small business capacity and leadership styles within the government contracting arena and how these dynamics relate to organizational performance. In particular, researchers addressed aspects related to the lack of small business participation in government contracting opportunities. Also addressed in scholarly literature was contractor performance outside of the field of government contracting. This scholarly literature that was independent from contracting, compared and contrast leadership theory or leadership styles related to performance and success.

The content within the *Public procurement Government contracting* included studies reviewed from 2011 to 2014 addressed each critical research question element. With the paucity of research on strategies for achieving positive performance in government contracts, the articles selected, taken both individually and mutually, did not offer a solution to the central research question. As previously mentioned, the structured literature review included an emphasis on each theme discussed as it related to a pertinent descriptive elements. Each relevant part was essential to answering the central research question of how perceived strategies facilitate positive performance in government contracting opportunities. Themes revealed included leadership's role in: (a) building collaborative working relationships, (b) aligning goals with the principal (federal level government agencies) to create value for both parties, and (c) implementing actions to create long-term value and growth. The importance of small business leaders maintaining positive performance in government contracting emerged as a significant problem because long-term ramifications exist for small businesses whose income relied solely on public contracting opportunities. The information gathered will help fill gaps in business research to couple with collected data to answer the question, What leadership strategies do small business leaders use to achieve positive performance ratings in government contracts?

Transition and Summary

Chapter 1 began with the foundation and background to cultivate and understand historically, how the business problem emerged as an important topic for research. The problem and purpose statements expanded the scope and purposefulness and indicated the direction of this study. The nature of the study included a brief objective for selecting a qualitative method and descriptive design. The research question and conceptual framework explained the central question and the theoretical lens. Operational definitions defined technical terms. Based on the descriptive paradigm, assumptions, limitations, and delimitations assisted in identifying and setting aside biases. The significant results from the study include detailed descriptions and value to businesses and contributions for improved business practices and positive social change. Chapter 2 was the academic literature review.

The results contain elements to fill gaps in literature on performance in government contracting opportunities. Chapter 3 provided greater understanding and rationale for the method, design and procedures followed to conduct the study using a systemic approach. Chapter 4 included the findings, discussion on the prospects for application in professional practice, and implications for social change.

CHAPTER III

METHODS AND PROCEDURES

The Project

Chapter 3 summarizes the research process for this qualitative descriptive study. The information serves as a roadmap in describing how the researcher explored strategies small business leaders may have used for positive performance ratings in government contracting. Restating the purpose, this chapter explains the researcher's role as a participant observer and data collection instrument. Participant selection method and design is discussed in detail. The discussion also includes how the researcher ensured data saturation. The population and sampling chapter justifies how and why the participants will benefit the study and explains the chosen sampling technique. Important details underlining a discussion expanding on ethical considerations and protecting participants' rights were outlined in this section. The data collection and data analysis processes followed Moustakas's (1994) modified van Kaam systemic approach to collecting and organizing data. The researcher conducted the study in accordance with the parameters established by Walden University's Institutional Review Board (IRB) to ensure the ethical protection of research participants. The approval number is 05-12-15-0481984, expiring May 11, 2016 (see appendix E). The process for ensuring reliability and validity throughout the study and a transition concludes this section.

Purpose Statement

The purpose of this qualitative descriptive research study was to explore strategies small business leaders used to attain positive performance ratings in government contracting. The researcher gained this understanding by interviewing small business leaders located within 30 miles of Washington, DC, with favorable CPARS (past performance ratings) on at least three government contracting opportunities. Implementing strategies that increased small business performance in government contracting influenced social change through enabling business leaders to create new jobs, increase contributions to the government tax base, and improve the well-being for the unemployed job base this group can employ.

Role of the Researcher

Qualitative methods include structured, exhaustive, holistic examinations of a phenomenon. The researcher's role involved obtaining evidence by the descriptive research processes and following a systemic method to collect, organize, and analyze information to answer the central research question (e.g., Moustakas, 1994; Shields & Rangarjan, 2013). The researcher ensured successful data attainment that did not compromise the U.S. Department of Health and Human Services (1974) regulations on the protecting human subjects. The researcher incorporated open-ended questions in the interview protocol to uncover as much about the participants and their situations as possible (Jacob & Furgerson, 2012). Following Leko's method (2014), using semi-structured interviews in natural settings with participants helped the researcher uncover unforeseen discoveries and opportunities for further exploration.

The descriptive focus through asking general questions about the perceptions and experience, gaining another's perspective, demands participants receive some information about the phenomenon from the researcher beforehand (Englander, 2012). With 13 years of federal experience, including nine years working as a warranted, government-contracting officer, the researcher had industry expertise from a government contracting officer's viewpoint with a professional connection the phenomenon. The researcher's responsibility as a contracting officer had included soliciting small businesses for government contracting opportunities. The researcher worked directly with Washington, DC, area business owners and leaders to facilitate positive working relationships between the government and contractors to meet established contractual and performance goals. The researcher was a contracting officer who maintained a Federal Acquisition Certification-Contracting Level III certification that awarded contracts and served as the lead negotiator and final contractor performance evaluator on government contracts.

The researcher's experience and professional involvement in government acquisitions created potential bias during data collection. The professional relationship with the target population increased the degree to which bias may have manifested. Insider investigators, such as academic researchers, tend to limit the scope of their inquiries only to discover what they think they do not know (Chenail, 2011). The researcher followed Chenail (2011) methodology and promoted objectivity by opening up questions to encompass what the researcher did not know to limit bias based on in-depth personal involvement in government procurement. Because qualitative research results include descriptive analyses that increased susceptibility to biases, an effort was made to ensure objectivity in data collection and interpretive analysis activities.

Participants

Participants were small business leaders, including CEOs, presidents, owners, or general managers, located within 30 miles of Washington, DC. To qualify to participate, business leaders required positive performance ratings on at least three procurement opportunities in the CPARS. As qualitative researchers (Sanjari, Bahramnezhad, Khoshnava Fomani, Shoghi, & Cheraghi, 2014) have demonstrated, in qualitative research, a researcher's involvement encompasses all stages of the study from defining a concept to design, interview, transcription, analysis, verification, and reporting the concepts and themes. In this study, the researcher's tasks involved finding and selecting participants who reported having experiences correlated with the phenomenon being studied, which for some studies can be a difficult task (e.g., Englander, 2012). Clear articulation of criteria existed to select participants. Standardized and pre-established criteria that dictated how to accomplish the task did not exist (Moustakas, 1994; Shields & Rangarjan, 2013).

To identify participants, the researcher searched for companies registered on Federal Business Opportunities (FBO), a public website and the federal government's primary Government Point of Entry (GPE) for all open-market contracting opportunities that exceeded $25,000 (FAR, 2014c). Every government contractor aspiring to conduct business with the federal government can register on this public website (https://www.fbo.gov). The FBO site provided a starting point to gather participants as it maintains data about contract awards and business classifications for each business receiving an award. The System for Award Management (SAM) database maintains information on all contractors that do business with the government. Every business must register with the system before any contract award could be awarded. The SAM database identified the North American Industry Classification System (NAICS) codes to determine and ensure the researcher included diverse socio-economic categories under the small business umbrella. The SBA's (2015) Dynamic Small Business Search Database and U.S. Department of Veterans Affairs (2015) Vendor Information Pages (online government websites) house publicly available contractor data also served as resources for finding participants from various socio-economic groups. The researcher focused on small businesses with at least three positive CPARS ratings. CPARS represents the government-wide electronic performance reporting for firms that perform in contracts awarded by the federal government agency or department. The system assists government contracting officials in ensuring the government does business with companies that could provide quality goods and services within budget and on time, providing deliverables by or before the contract designated deadlines (GAO, 2013). The preliminary questions distributed required participants to exhibit knowledge of CPARS and identify contracts awarded to them resulting in positive CPARS database reports (see Appendix C).

The researcher invited members to participate through e-mail communication (see Appendix A). E-mail assists in expanding recruitment when research information is accessible by posting e-mail requests for participants on relevant websites (Cook, 2012). Recruiting participants online helps researchers by eliminating the constraints and barriers to reach participants with valid, highly specialized knowledge (Brandon, Long, Loraas, Mueller-Phillips, & Vansant, 2014). Using e-mail requests to recruit participants capitalized on a shared resource that served as a significant component to business owners (Truong et al., 2013). Screening questions probed during solicitation ensured participants met criteria for participation, as well as identified socio-economic demographic categories (see Appendix C). The socio-economic identified related to the business meeting certain classification standards as defined and established by SBA definitions. A preliminary telephone conversation with each respondent helped establish a working relationship. Interviewees required time to warm up when beginning the interviews and establishing a rapport enhanced the comfort level when they were speaking with the researcher (J. Smith et al., 2011). The goal was to have a conversation that evolved into thematic expressions through collaborative interaction (Van Manen, 1990). The collaborative interaction allowed probing for an elaborate explanation or the exploration of new themes that may have emerged during the interview (Doody & Noonan, 2013). Establishing a working relationship and providing preparation information before the meeting increased the chances for sincere responses of comprehensive accounts from participants.

Research Method and Design

The chosen method and design for the research was a qualitative descriptive study. The method and design developed from the business problem statement, which indicated the study would involve a qualitative descriptive exploration to understand strategies that contribute to small businesses' positive performance ratings in government contracts. The following sub-sections include descriptions and rationales for implementing specified research methodology and design strategy for conducting this study.

Method

Successful qualitative research features notable descriptions for method selection (Bansal & Corley, 2012). Qualitative research methods have their origins in social and behavioral sciences and serve to explore human science research and leadership behavior to understand the phenomenon (Moustakas, 1994; Shield, & Rangarjan, 2013). Researchers use the qualitative method to help uncover unanticipated findings or avenues for further exploration through facilitating open-ended investigations (Leko, 2014). The method selected to explore participants' lived experiences helped bridge gaps in performance and leadership research and its role in government contracting.

Advantages existed for conducting qualitative research as opposed to mixed-methods or quantitative research. For this research study, the primary advantage was the ability to bring understanding to business issues involving human values and beliefs (W. Gordon, 2011). Mixed methods research in leadership provides a way to advance theory (Stentz, Plano Clark, & Matkin, 2012). This research study lends to an exploratory design to understand how successful leaders function in small businesses, but not research to advance theory.

Although mixed-methods research was a viable option for leadership research, qualitative research was the most suitable for this study type. A purely quantitative approach may not have captured the cultural contexts and vast leadership topics that qualitative research fosters (Stentz et al., 2012). The qualitative method involved highlighting perceptions of participants who had experience the phenomenon, which corroborated the reason for selecting the qualitative method over the quantitative or mixed-method designs to conduct the study.

Research Design

Business and academic research involves observing applied principles practiced by analyzing viewpoints relative to new perspectives. As a result, the descriptive research design emerged as an appropriate qualitative method for investigating business phenomena in this academic research study. Knowledge comes from the individual's perceptions, focusing on discovering the nature of specific events to establish meaning to a phenomenon (Lambert & Lambert, 2012; Moustakas,

1994). The researcher becomes more interested in instances or essences than the factual status (Van Manen, 1990). This study's researcher chose a descriptive design for this academic study for the factual status descriptors. The research design selection afforded a juncture to unveil what participants perceived as strategies that facilitated positive government contractor performance. Using emerging questions allowed the required data retrieval from participants' viewpoint (Moustakas, 1994). Exploring lived human experience, the researcher described how performance strategies manifested in small business leaders to identify, and elaborate on, the phenomenon's essential structures (Sousa, 2014). Descriptive research involves applying thematic analysis to detect actual behavior, attitudes, or real motives of the people being studied (Vaismoradi, Turunen, & Bondas, 2013). Elements revealed from extrapolating personal knowledge from the participants helped the researcher understand the phenomenon enabling exploration for solutions viable for practical use in the government contracting industry.

A phenomenological study was less appropriate than other qualitative designs for investigating the business phenomenon. Ethnographic research design had potential for the study. However, the intent did not include immersing the reseacher in a social situation by probing the everyday lives, conduct, and societal movements as a whole (A. Brown & Iacono, 2012). The design facilitates understanding how groups and their individual members see themselves, and how the phenomenon affects them as a group. This study did not explore how groups and the groups' individual members saw themselves. A narrative design was not suitable because the approach provided an advantageous tactic for describing an individual's life story that is not conducive to obtaining perspectives from groups or organizations as a whole (Gill, 2014). Case study designs are most suitable for studying complex systems in business research because they allow for data collection from multiple levels, perspectives, and sources over an extended period (Yin, 2009). The research focus limited a case study design as it lacked the capacity to integrate and explore complex systems. In grounded theory, researchers construct theories based on collected data as opposed to interpreting phenomena to obtain an exact picture. As an approach that involves an attempt to develop a theory, the grounded theory method did not provide the appropriate opportunity to collect data with the rigor expected for the study.

Population and Sampling

Through qualitative inquiry, the researcher used purposeful sampling to ensure the appropriate population contributed to answering the central research question. Any purposeful sampling technique could have been used in a qualitative descriptive design (Lambert & Lambert, 2012). In purposeful sampling in qualitative studies, the researcher selected participants who had pertinent information on the subject to help understand the phenomenon explored (Suri, 2011). The sample of business leaders selected ensured participants understood the topic under study and had valuable perspectives (i.e., Robinson, 2013). Following Moustakas' method (1994), interviewing 21 participants proved important for purposeful sampling to ensure adequate participants within the population understood the phenomenon through their lived experiences. The target population was small business leaders, defined as CEOs, presidents, owners, or general managers who had completed at least three government procurement opportunities that had received positive past performance ratings. Interviewing leaders employed by companies with positive past performance ratings as determined by a contracting officer helped identify themes in business strategies as they pertained to small business performance and government contracting opportunities. The target population and sample size was critical to answering the central question and exploring strategies that facilitate successful small businesses performance in government contracting opportunities.

The qualitative descriptive study involved semi-structured interviews with at least 20 small business leaders. The critical criterion were the participants required business leadership experience helped to ensure they had lived the experience (Moustakas, 1994). When identifying participants, the aim was for potential selectees to have at least a general knowledge about the phenomenon. Knowledgeable participants potentially offer experienced insight into the general structure even with their identities protected (Englander, 2012).

Communicating perceptions from participants who had lived the experience provided significance to outcomes, accounts, and data quality (Bansal & Corley, 2012). The interview place and setting were necessary, as the consideration could have affected the relationship between the interviewer and the participant and data collection (Doody & Noonan, 2013). Following

Moustakas' method (1994), the researcher created an environment where the participant sensed enough comfort to share openly and honestly. Interviews were conducted at a location of the participant's choosing or over a securely recorded telephone line. Ideally, the locale had little background noise to minimize distraction, allow for precise recording, and foster a safe and nonthreatening environment for the participant (Jacob & Furgerson, 2012). For this study, a familiar setting to the participant or a mutually agreed meeting place offered the most advantageous environment conducive to sharing.

Interviewing 21 participants ensured saturation. Saturation, along with other factors, determined the qualitative sample size was sufficient to yield balanced, complete, and trustworthy data findings. Saturation is the point at which a researcher determines that no new thematic codes exist (Morse, Lowery, & Steury, 2014). Data saturation is the point where the interviewer has obtained sufficient information from the field and interviews cease to reveal new data (Coenen, Stamm, Stucki, & Cieza, 2012). Sufficient interview information meant no new thematic coding occurs, and the study could be replicable. Saturation was appropriate for this descriptive study because it contains an ideal guideline for purposive sampling, as discussed in the Population and Sampling section (e.g., J. L. Walker, 2012). A high likelihood exists for reaching saturation when the participants selected are rich in information that leads to the uncovering of events experienced (Lambert & Lambert, 2012). No single factor existed that dictated the saturation rate using qualitative data collection methods. Therefore, to increase the chance of achieving saturation, the researcher continued interviews until no new information was obtained from the 21 participants.

Ethical Research

To ensure adherence to ethical considerations, the researcher began by completing an applicable training course in ethical principles in research from the National Institutes of Health Office of Extramural Research (2013) Human Research Protections (see Appendix B). Ethical principles guided how human science researchers interact with participants (Moustakas, 1994). Researchers have a responsibility to ensure the adherence to ethical practices (Vanclay, Baines, & Taylor, 2013). Identified issues pertinent to the study required were communicated to the IRB to establish a plan to manage them. While completing the IRB form, the researcher directed attention to identified principles that addressed ethical concerns explicit to the topic.

Details such as the given location, participation time, population, instrument used for data collection, and methodology emerged as relevant facts identified to the IRB. The procedures for obtaining subjects' voluntary informed consent included a step-by-step process for subjects to withdraw from the study, keeping participants anonymous, and assuring participants' confidentiality protection ensured adherence to ethical principles. The process followed the ethical principle of justice, which involves bearing the burdens and receiving the benefits of research. A checklist included information regarding the release of results to the subjects explained how the researcher intend to use the data collected. The researcher identified participants by assigned ID numbers to protect anonymity and maintained the data in a safe place for five years to safeguard participant's confidentiality. After five years, the researcher will destroy all consent forms and interview documentation. Vanclay et al. (2013) noted many principles maintain general and universal applicability throughout research. The summarized steps below, as outlined in the informed consent, ensured adherence to ethical principles:

1. The researcher fully disclosed the purpose and use of this study to participants.
2. The researcher obtained informed consent in writing from participants.
3. A volunteer could withdraw by writing and signing their intention to withdraw on the consent form.
4. As a voluntary study, the researcher did not offer incentives for participation.
5. The researcher will maintain the data in a safe place for five years.
6. The findings do not include participant's names, titles, or company names.

Data Collection

This study involved exploring strategies small business leaders use to attain positive performance in government contracting through a descriptive qualitative examination. Descriptive research requires collecting data in a methodical manner to satisfy requirements (Lambert & Lambert, 2012). The requirements included developing questions to guide the interview process, collecting data, and organizing the data in a systemic way (Moustakas, 1994). The following three sections details data collection methods to answer the central question: the (a) data collection instrument, (b) data collection technique, and (c) data organization techniques.

Data Collection Instrument

The data collection instrument included a 10-minute researcher developed a pre-interview questionnaire for qualifying prospective participants to gather socio-economic data (see Appendix C) and a general pre-interview questionnaire to obtain perceptions of perceived strategies small business leaders use to attain positive performance ratings in government contracting. As an interviewer, the researcher served as the primary data collection instrument to obtain information through open-ended interview questions the researcher developed for the study (see Appendix D).

Typical data collection methods in descriptive qualitative research include interviews and the most common involve semi-structured interviews (Kahlke,

2014). Comparable to naturalistic conversation, semi-structured interviews allow a rapport – communication between friends – that allows the participant to recount their life experience (J. A. Smith et al., 2009; Madill, 2011). The researcher used semi-structured open-ended interviews with predetermined questions through which participants could provide full descriptions of their experiences. The instrument chosen allowed a flexible forum for communication to substantiate the lived experiences and understand how small businesses leaders perceive strategies that facilitated positive performance ratings in government contracting. Semi-structured open-ended interviews involving business leaders were a viable option for exploring leadership behavior (Bublak, 2014; Holloway, 2013). The researcher developed interview guide (see Appendix D) to increase the opportunity to facilitate a comfortable interaction that enabled participants to provide an exhaustive account of their experiences (e.g., J. A. Smith et al., 2009). Pre-determined questions allowed the freedom to explore issues that arose spontaneously and sought clarification when required (e.g., Doody & Noonan, 2013). The data collection questions included a script (see Appendix D) as a reminder to share critical details about the study and explain informed consent (e.g., Jacob & Furgerson, 2012). General questions designed to collect participants' detailed views helped the researcher interpret the interviewees' communicated meaning. The questions resulted in extensive description extraction from participants' lived experiences.

Data verification and the ability to replicate such studies by reassessing the findings in different contexts are important considerations for researchers. Reliability includes the measure of consistency. The use of strategies employed to measure reliability depends on how the data is collected, and how the findings will be analyzed (Fan & Sun, 2014). Descriptive qualitative researchers achieve data reliability by establishing the dependability through peer review and consensus of respondents' themes (Kisely & Kendall, 2011). The participants previewed the data collection instrument before the interview to prepare. After the interview, participants reviewed the data from their interviews to make additions or corrections.

Validity exists as the most fundamental concern in any measurement situation (Fan & Sun, 2014) and signifies the robustness and accuracy of findings generated (Mangioni & McKerchar, 2013). Validity is essential because it addressed the accuracy of research results (Moustakas, 1994). An advantageous method for ensuring data validity in qualitative research involved transcription review (Kisely & Kendall, 2011; Moustakas, 1994; Thomas & Magilvy, 2011). Transcript review method ensures accuracy in recording what the participant stated by allowing the interviewees to review independently their interview transcripts and discuss and/or correct any discrepancies (Kisely & Kendall, 2011). The data collection method using semi-structured interviews served as an additional legitimacy. The participant's final analysis assessment for accuracy and concurrence assisted in ensuring truthful account and intended meaning of perceived experiences.

Data Collection Technique

Small business representatives solicited for notification via e-mail were identified through public contact information retrieved from the Federal Business Opportunities (FBO), System for Award Management (SAM), Dynamic Small Business Search (DSBS), and Vendor Information Pages (VIP) websites. Following Englander's methodology (2012), face-to-face and telephone interviews emerged as the most suitable techniques to obtain the depth required for this qualitative study. Disadvantages to conducting face-to-face interviews include participants not having the time or calendar availability to devote to the study to discuss their experiences or not being comfortable with participating in an audio-recorded interview (Doody & Noonan, 2013). Constraints exist in finding and reaching participants willing to participate, but electronic correspondence helped eliminate these restrictions (Brandon et al., 2014). An inexperienced or novice data collector may collect unusable data because they poorly manage and conduct interviews (Van Manen, 1990). Other problems novices encounter include challenges remembering issues, remaining focused, and accidentally leading the participants (J. A. Smith et al., 2009). While disadvantages existed for the data collection technique, many advantages also existed. For example, conducting semi-structured interviews allow the data collector to change the order of questions if required or if the flow of conversation warrants (Doody & Noonan, 2013). The technique provides an opportunity to obtain richer nuances and fruitful responses from participants (Englander, 2012). Adequate question and interview structure permitted an interviewer to evoke a comprehensive account of participants lived experiences (Moustakas, 1994). The strengths for conducting semi-structured, open-ended interviews face-to-face or by telephone outweigh the weaknesses. The following paragraphs describe the technique used to collect data through a step-by-step process. The first four steps applied to the interview preparation phase, followed by the interview process phase and then the transcript review process.

First, potential participants with high specialist knowledge received an invitation to participate via e-mail (see Appendix A). E-mail recruitment increased access to interviewees (Brandon et al., 2014). The screening questions developed by the researcher ensured volunteer participants met the minimum criteria for participation (see Appendix C).

Second, a preliminary telephone conversation with each respondent established a working relationship. The goal was to make them comfortable with sharing their experience openly and honestly (Moustakas, 1994; J. A. Smith et al., 2009; Van Manen, 1990).

Third, following the confirmation of a commitment, the respondents received critical details of the study and interview questions. An explanation of informed consent provided the details necessary to assist in preparing for the interview (e.g., Doody & Noonan, 2013; Jacob & Furgerson, 2012).

Fourth, there was an agreement on a safe, relatively quiet, nonthreatening environment for the interview of the participant's choice (e.g., Jacob & Furgerson, 2012).

Fifth, during the interview process, the pre-determined questions allowed the researcher the freedom to explore issues that arose spontaneously and the ability to search for clarification when required (e.g., Doody & Noonan, 2013). Following Jacob & Furgerson methodology, (2012) the researcher developed a script (see Appendix D) that served as a reminder and task list to ask pertinent questions, share critical details, and address important interview elements. Recording devices and light journaling were used to collect information from the interviews for transcription during the data organization phase. Volunteers were likely to agree to audio recording during the interview, although it may take them time to feel comfortable about speaking freely (Doody & Noonan, 2013). Recording data strictly by writing notes may cause a novice interviewer to miss critical details reported by participants' (Doody & Noonan, 2013). The researcher only created a written record noting key terms and audio recordings to ensure detailed accounts to gave accurate meaning to participants' experiences (e.g., Bansal & Corley, 2012).

The sixth and final step involved a transcript review. Moustakas (1994) suggested researchers validate collected data by having participants examine the descriptions. Reliability occurs by establishing data dependability through peer-review and consensus (Kisely & Kendall, 2011). To ensure process validity (Fan & Sun, 2014), robustness, and accuracy (Mangioni & McKerchar, 2013), the researcher provided participants with transcribed data to review, correct and approve before organizing and analyzing.

Data Organization Techniques

In qualitative research, data organization begins when the researcher receives transcripts and contemplates the methods and procedures for analysis (Moustakas, 1994). Researchers have an obligation to act with integrity, be fair, conduct their research properly, avoid conflicts of interest, and minimize moral hazards (Vanclay et al., 2013). Keeping a research log helped record insights gained from reflection or discerning patterns (e.g., Moustakas, 1994). The regular recording of descriptions and commentaries proved helpful when analyzing data (J. A. Smith et al., 2009). Following White, Oelke, and Friesen (2012) this researcher used electronic matrices using the NVivo system to organize data for theming, visual displays, streamlined summarization, and simplification in reorganization. The NVivo software contains tools assisted the researcher to manage and organize data (Sotiriadou, Brouwers, & Le, 2014). Software is appropriate for both documentation and to develop systematic folder structures and file naming conventions (Margarian, 2014). The transcribed documents were imported directly into the software and organized through researcher-developed folders. The folders contained labels identifying themes and participant perspectives. Organized records and information was remaindered in a secure location to protect the participants. Information housed on a computer contained secure password protection. Transcripts and non-secure information did not include identification information. The researcher kept all raw data in a secure and protected location for five years, after which all the materials and data were destroyed.

Data Analysis Technique

Qualitative researchers must devise creative ways to present their data because qualitative data are not readily conducive to synthesis or reduction into tables (Bansal & Corley, 2012). The moment the researcher receives transcribed interviews, the data organization process begins (Moustakas, 1994). For a descriptive study, the researcher determined how the data are organized (Lambert & Lambert, 2012). Moustakas (1994) created an applicable philosophical framework for qualitative research. Therefore, using NVivo to pinpoint themes and provide annotation for codes and categories, the researcher used Moustakas's (1994) modified van Kaam method data analysis to organize and analyze the information. Moustakas's (1994) modified van Kaam method analysis included seven steps to code, group and cluster transcribed interview data collected from participants into major themes. Summarized into five steps, procedures included: (a) extrapolating horizontalized statements relative to the question, (b) using horizontalized statements to list the units of meaning, (c) clustering units into themes, (d) develop textural descriptions of experience into clustered themes, and finally (e) integrating textural descriptions into meaning and essence (Moustakas, 1994).

Matrices served as a means to extract and guide themes into a visual display (White et al., 2012). Attention to familiar terms from significant topics identified in the literature review and conceptual framework helped compose major themes for analysis. The analysis phase included published literature since the writing the proposal to offer new information and help complete the comprehensive analysis with information published within the same year. NVivo data analysis software was suitable for compiling and clustering data. The software provided a critical view, serves to interpret the data, and provides a way to draw conclusions about the findings to tell a story (e.g. Sotiriadou, Brouwers, & Le, 2014). NVivo provided the best opportunity to gain an accurate account of perceived small business leaders' experience that had been effective in employing strategies leading to positive performance ratings in government contracts.

Reliability and Validity

Establishing quality in a doctoral study involved ensuring articulated finding exist mutual reliability and validity. A significant perceived weakness exists in qualitative inquiry centered on research validity and reliability (Mangioni & McKerchar, 2013). Techniques to improve quality included objective transcript reviews combined with meetings with participants to discuss inconsistencies to attain accord (Kisely & Kendall, 2011).

The researcher used the study design to determine how to improve quality. The two essential parameters for establishing quality were reliability and validity. Researchers used methods retrieved from existing qualitative research that had established different criteria to assess the rigor. Reliability and validity have been uncertain and in many instances not applicable in qualitative research (Sinkovics & Alfoldi, 2012). The researcher used the most common methods to check reliability and validity as proposed by Lincoln and Guba (1985): credibility, dependability, confirmability, and transferability. The subsequent sections include steps taken to address and achieve rigor in this qualitative descriptive study.

Credibility

Credibility in qualitative research encompasses elements of validity and reliability denoting the findings value and believability (Lincoln & Guba 1985). Lincoln and Guba (1985) suggested four strategies to address credibility: prolonged engagement and persistent observation, triangulation, peer debriefing, and transcription review. Prolonged engagement and persistent observation gathered from multiple sources increases research credibility (Houghton, Casey, Shaw, & Murphy, 2013). Ensuring credibility using these methods requires researchers to spend sufficient time ensuring the data collected from participant experiences embraced a full understanding.

Different frameworks help researchers achieve credibility. Following J. Gordon and Patterson (2013), the researcher proliferated credibility through a combination of in-depth interviews with activities and artifacts such as non-proprietary documents that add depth and richness. The measures described increased plausibility that would not have been complete if the researcher only conducted interviews. The researcher collaborated with industry practitioners, such as small business leaders, who had successfully performed in government contracting opportunities (e.g., Yang et al., 2010).

Transferability

Transferability refers to the degree to which a researcher shows findings have applicability in other contexts or settings. In qualitative research, transferability also refers to generalizability through thoroughly describing context and assumptions central to the analysis (Lincoln & Guba, 1985). Research users and applicable professionals are in a better position than the researcher to determine where to transfer the results of this study. Generalizability serves as a comprehensive framework for measuring reliability and validity by encompassing other methods (Fan & Sun, 2014).

Qualitative researchers could enhance transferability by thoroughly describing the research context and the assumptions (Lincoln & Guba, 1985). Schou, Høstrup, Lyngsø, Larsen, and Poulsen (2012) studied questions in qualitative research that increased instances for transferability in study conclusions. The researcher strived for generalizability by ensuring thoroughness in context descriptions.

Thoroughness included vigorous content account, with examples and appropriate quotations from interview transcripts to allow readers to consider their interpretations (Houghton et al., 2013). Three elements identified helped the audience understand the reasons and methods behind the careful selection of informed and experienced participants. The three components included: (a) descriptions of participant selection decision, (b) the context for connection to research, and (c) the relationship between the researcher's knowledge and the phenomenon (e.g., Schou et al., 2012). Careful consideration of each element above increased reliability and validity through a cumulative attempt to set the stage for research users and professionals who might have considered transferring the findings to other platforms.

Dependability

Dependability refers to producing similar interpretations from all participants (White et al., 2012). Dependability occurs by accounting for changing settings and describing how the changes influence or alter how a researcher approached a study (Lincoln & Guba, 1985). For example, when conducting interviews, an interviewer may respond differently to each participant, often as a reaction to interviewees' demeanor and comfort level (Rodham, Fox, & Doran, 2013). The steps identified in subsequent paragraphs will increase methodology replication with a larger population or by future researchers.

The data collection technique requires thoroughly describing strategic level planning to adjust to changing contexts that occur within research (White et al., 2012). When coding the transcribed data, the researcher used searches for multiple words or phrases containing the same meaning to capture key phrases. Using multiple searches assisted in adjustments for differences in dialect among participants to ensure accurate accounts by noting key semantic relationships (White et al., 2012). As an independent researcher, the researcher examined both the process and the product to evaluate accuracy and determined whether the data supported the findings, interpretations, and conclusions (e.g., Lincoln & Guba, 1985). An audit trail documented changes that occurred in addition to any adjustments to the researcher's approach throughout the process (e.g., Lincoln & Guba,

1985). Finally, explaining subsequent factors that affected outcomes provided a clear framework to produce the same results when replicating.

Confirmability

Confirmability closely correlated to dependability because both concepts required the researcher to document changes in processes for transparency and replicability. Confirmabilty referred to the degree to which one can substantiate the results. Maintaining an auditing trail in both the data collection and analysis demonstrated accurate, comprehensive records of approaches and activities employed (White et al., 2012). Perpetuating an auditable footprint allowed for dialog between the researcher and the data that facilitated a truthful representation of activities throughout the data analysis process (e.g., Rodham et al., 2013). The selected means for ensuring confirmability allowed the researcher to grasp shortcomings and contradictions to check and recheck the data throughout the study. Participants reviewed transcribed data for accuracy (Kisely & Kendall, 2011). As identified in addressing dependability, an independent researcher examined the data to help substantiate interpretations and conclusions (Lincoln & Guba, 1985). Using audit trails provided a substantial methodological reference that satisfied the intent to ensure the selected framework, themes, methodology, and interpretations fell within the context to which they belong.

Transition and Summary

The information discussed in Chapter 3 outlined methods used to conduct this qualitative descriptive study to exploring strategies some small business leaders use to attain positive performance ratings in government contracting.

Chapter 1 served as the foundation for the study. Chapter 1 included the problem and purpose statements, nature of the study, research question, conceptual framework, and a discussion of listed and defined operational definitions. To identify and help set aside bias, Chapter 1 addressed assumptions, limitations, delimitations, and significance, and detailed explanations addressing value and application to business processes.

Chapter 2 contained a thorough literature review

for exploring strategies that facilitate positive past performance ratings in government contracting opportunities. The foundation and background prescribed accounted for the business problem history.

Chapter 3 detailed the systemic process for exploring strategies small business leaders use to attain positive performance ratings in government contracting by understanding small business leaders' experiences. This section began with restating the purpose and describing my role as the researcher. The discussion on participant selection allowed for greater understanding and rationale for the sampled groups that contributed by providing significant accounts of their experience. The Research Methodology and Design section included reasonings for selecting and using the identified strategy. The Population and Sampling section included a discussion on how and why the population interviewed was suitable for the study and details about the sampling technique used. Ethical considerations underlined the actions taken to protect participants' rights during the data collection, analysis, and presentation phases. The data collection and data analysis subsections emphasized the systemic approach to collecting, analyzing, and organizing data. This section concluded with outlining the actions used to ensure reliability and validity throughout the study.

CHAPTER IV

FINDINGS, SUMMARY, CONCLUSIONS, AND RECOMMENDATIONS

Application to Professional Practice and Implications for Change

Chapter 1 provided a foundation and background of the study, which introduced the topic and problem chosen to solve the applied business problem. The review of the literature provided an immersing discussion into the literature pertaining to the problem was in Chapter 2. Chapter 3 summarized the entire research process commissioned to conduct the qualitative descriptive study. Chapter 4 identified themes and summarizes leadership strategies small business owners used for positive performance ratings in the federal contracting arena. This section included the delivery of a presentation and report of the findings from the data gathered. Chapter 4 concluded with the impact these findings have on social change and a plan of action for practitioners to practically apply information the study availed.

Introduction

The purpose of this qualitative descriptive research study was to explore strategies small business leaders used to attain positive performance ratings in government contracting. The gathering of interview data from small business leaders in the Washington, DC, metropolitan area revealed five overall themes associated with the findings from the study. These themes included: (a) leadership strategies that influence positive performance ratings, (b) behavioral or trait-based attributes of leaders, (c) understanding bureaucratic dynamics and contract requirements, (d) resource-based capacity as an impediment, and (e) competitive intelligence as a valuable resource. The analysis of the themes of the study revealed that behavioral, value-based, and trait-based leadership characteristics are essential in leading government contracts. The leadership behaviors described by participants based on their experiences closely aligned with both transformational and servant leadership. The researcher also found bureaucratic structure and system and past employment or project performance of the contractors influenced the positive procurement process and performance ratings among government contractors. The sub-theme of communication appeared to be an important factor in understanding the needs of the clients, which is essential to gaining trust and confidence. These elements supported the need for the contractors to establish a positive working relationship with government agencies.

Presentation of the Findings

The qualitative descriptive research questions constructed developed an understanding of leadership strategies small business leaders deemed successful in facilitating positive performance rating for their organizations while performing on government contracts. Data was obtained to answer the central question: What leadership strategies do small business leaders use to achieve positive performance ratings in government contracts? The data provided the information around which the following sections were structured. This question was explored using the following 10 interview questions posed to 21 leaders during face-to-face interviews:

Q1: What leadership strategies do you find most effective for achieving positive performance ratings in government contracts?

Q2: What leadership behaviors do leaders/managers employ that are attributes to positive performance ratings in government contracts?

Q3: How do these attributes influence contract performance ratings?

Q4: How does the contractor–government relationship impede or affect performance ratings?

Q5: What are the impediments or obstacles that small business leaders face when performing in government contracts?

Q6: What resources do business leaders use to assist in achieving positive performance ratings in government contracts?

Q7: What restrictions, if any, discourage small business representatives from achieving positive performance ratings in government contracting opportunities?

Q8: What additional information can you provide to improve leadership effectiveness in small businesses' contracting performance?

Q9: What programs and information will help leaders of small businesses seeking to improve performance ratings in government contracts?

Q10: What programs or information do you suggest to leaders of small businesses seeking to obtain government-contracting opportunities?

In seeking answers to the central research question, five themes emerged in the thematic analysis performed for the 21 interview transcripts. These themes included: (a) leadership strategies that influence positive performance ratings, (b) behavioral or trait-based attributes of leaders, (c) understanding bureaucratic dynamics and contract requirements, (d) resource-based capacity as an impediment, and (e) competitive intelligence as a valuable resource. In the following section, the researcher presented the themes and sub-themes with verbatim textual support from the participants.

Theme 1: Leadership Strategies that Influence Positive Performance Ratings

Theme 1 emerged from the aggregation of 11 sub-themes or the thematic categories explaining the strategies for positive performance. These sub-themes included: (a) perseverance of organizational leadership, (b) communication skills of contractors, (c) emotional intelligence of project managers, (d) business insights, (e) good understanding of the bureaucracy, (f) demonstration of long-term quality performance and effective working relationship, (g) continuous organizational improvement, (h) accountability of actions and commitments, (i) integrity of the organization, (j) competitiveness, and (k) available mentors (see Table 2). The necessity to manage identified relational dynamics of social, political, legal, and behavioral dynamics expressed by participants in Theme 1 included its sub-themes aligned with elements defined by Fayezi et al. (2012), where insights for relationship engineering within supply chains were found to dominate. Each theme is presented and substantiated in this section.

Table 1 - Leadership Strategies that Influence Positive Performance Ratings

Sub-themes	No. of occurrence	% of occurrence
Perseverance of organizational leadership	16	76
Effective Communication skills of contractors	14	67
Demonstration of long-term quality performance and effective working relationship	6	29
Emotional intelligence of project managers	6	29
Business insights of leaders	5	24
Good understanding of the bureaucracy	5	24
Continuous organizational improvement	2	10
Accountability of actions and commitment	2	10
Integrity of the organization	2	10
Competitiveness	2	10
Availability of mentors	1	5

Perseverance of organizational leadership. This sub-theme received 16 out of the 21 total sample population or 76%. Participant 10 talked about the perseverance character of a leader. Participant 10 defined a leader who perseveres as someone who keeps on trying despite experiencing failures. Participant 10 further described this character as the ability of a person to "deal with rejection and failures." Participant 10 also described perseverance as a work attitude. Participant 10 justified,

> Being a hard worker, being able to just keep going when things are tough. A lot of people want to call it quits or just don't have the work ethic. I think that if you want to be successful, you have to have that work ethic. You have to have that drive, just to keep working.

This leadership attitude related to procurement in the government as a process that typically observed specification, vendor selection, contracting, ordering, expediting, and evaluation (Miemczyk et al., 2012). Along with the observance of this process, contractors were obligated to comply with mandated compliance accreditations and documentation of past successful services that would support their history of competency to provide future (needed) contract services. The participants in the study reported that being persistent to comply with the requirements means engaging in trade-offs to win the contract, to meet performance measures, and potentially to acquire more future contract projects. This observation has been cited as the norm in government procurement activities (Lu, 2013; Miemczyk et al., 2012).

Participant 15, a female leader, used the term "tenacity" to define the perseverance of the leader in "withstand[ing] all the rejection along the way." The participants who identified persistence to continuously engage in the procurement process without the assurance of winning the service contracts believed with the routine practice of the federal government to engage in service contracting, even small and less competent contractors can acquire government projects. For Participant 16, a female leader, leaders in this business must jump legal hurdles and entertain contractual engagement to "secure either your certifications or the contracts themselves." Participant 16 stated, "Every single time, I believe, you will experience at least one setback. Most of them unexpected." Participant 16 shared how she managed project refusals that sometimes are offensive:

... to be successful, you have to continue
regardless of how you may feel about fairness
or accuracy in the rejections. My experience
was that when I was being certified, I would be
rejected at every turn and, with those
rejections, things would be said that were
absolutely not true and sometimes offensive. I
had to just continue, not talk about it with
everybody and disengage, but rather remain
engaged, quickly respond, and continue on the
path. I think that too many people stop when
they are hurt or when things are really hard or
unfair. They believe there's nothing you can do
and you just stop, but I believe that there's
always something you can do and you just
keep going.

Participant 15 stressed that perseverance is
associated with "confidence in yourself to know that you
can offer the government something they need that will
help them." This means the longer the contractor
demonstrated abilities to provide service, the higher the
chance the business could win future government
projects. Participant 15 said perseverance of a leader
can be observed in the following manner: "multi-tasking,

having the ability to juggle all the phases of obtaining work, performing work, monitoring personnel, monitoring contracts, just juggling all the balls that are required." As long as these competencies are demonstrated, they believed they would be selected to undertake certain contract projects.

Perseverance can be considered a legitimate strategy in the successful performance of government service contracts because awarding of government contracts does not observe service-based competition (Joaquin & Greitens, 2012; Johnston & Girth, 2012). This means contractors who may not be necessarily competent, but are available to provide service out of an urgency that could benefit the government agency from this procurement system. Leaders who are engaged in the contracting business may need to demonstrate they can provide service at the most convenient time and urgent needs of the procurement officials (Johnston & Girth, 2012).

Participant 19, a male leader, also explained that persistence is a prerequisite attitude of leaders who engaged in bureaucracy. He described the government transactions have several setbacks. He said, "There's just a lot of bureaucratic challenges and you have to be able to roll with those and move forward and you have to be able to inspire other people to follow you and persevere despite these things." The case of Participant 19 showed a typical long-term project requiring thorough reviews and evaluation of service activities and expected outcomes. Long-term and large projects are often confronted with bureaucratic challenges, which could take several months and years for contracts to be awarded. Participant 6, a female leader, shared that leaders must have the perseverance to undergo the government processes:

> Perseverance would be the first factor that comes up, and having faith. It is a slow process. They make it very clear, 18-24 months is kind of what they put out there to new businesses to say this process can be up to 18-24 months before you obtain federal business. There are many small businesses that have gone beyond that date in their efforts to obtain government contracts.

Effective communication skills of contractors. In the second sub-theme, 16 participants, or 67% (see Table 2), identified the uniqueness of government officials and the ability to exhibit varying communication styles as a strategy to success. Participant 11 associated effective management to the communication skills of the leader. Participant 11 described this skill as the ability of leaders to engage in open dialogue where expectations of the job are articulated. Participant 11 offered a strategy in demonstrating effective communication with the client. He said,

> One of the things I find that's helpful is having a schedule of deliverables. A plan of action and milestones that you review with the client regularly. That way there is no expectation differences between what the client thinks they're going to get and what you're going to provide. I think that's probably the most vital piece there. I've seen a lot of times with other companies where there's a total mismatch and the government client gets very upset and they say, "I'm never going to give any more work to this contractor again because they didn't deliver what I wanted." I think a lot of that is just tied to communication, and regular communication.

Several studies confirmed effective communication influences healthy working relationships, particularly in engagements requiring collaboration between two or more stakeholders (Grudinschi et al., 2014). Collaboration and partnerships were components identified as fundamental to public service procurement in previous research (Grudinschi et al., 2014); this study provided evidence that leaders may need to strengthen the communication system to maintain a successful collaborative relationship (Plane & Green, 2012).

Communication skill of leader is also demonstrated in dealing with the subordinates. Participant 11 shared that leaders should communicate to their staff the "deliverables and expectations from the client." He also shared that communication is necessary in ensuring employees coordinate effectively in providing the needs of the client. He said, "I think communication is key in making sure you support the client and then also support your staff." Participant 11 said employees should be aware that in the "contract environment ... you can lose your job the next day just because your contract comes to an end." Participant 11 stressed the following:

If you have your people in mind and you keep them informed of where you are in the lifecycle of the contract, and what you're doing to try to secure the next follow on contract, or what information you may need from them to make sure you win more work so they can continue employment with your company.

Participant 2, a male leader, explained communication skills were essential for leaders to articulate their vision, mission, and goals to subordinates, as well as the organization. Participant 2 figuratively used examples of miscommunication in the NASA mission to illustrate the need for leaders to communicate in order to complete the mission. He said, "So a leader has to be able to communicate that from top to bottom so that everyone buys into it."

Demonstration of long-term quality performance and effective working relationship. Six participants, or 29% (see Table 2), stressed that long-term quality performance and an effective working relationship are related and that leaders who were longtime contractors of the government projects have good understanding of the government working environment. Participant 18, a female leader, shared that for most of their government contracts, "relationship, quality of service and making a difference are the most effective for long term relationship and positive performance ratings." Participant 1, a male leader, added it is "helpful to have a good understanding of what these different people's perspectives and motivations are in there so that you can work together." Participant 1 added there are novice contractors who had performance issues because of their inability to consider the perspectives of the government officials. Participant 11 said,

> Where they have a really narrow view only from their own perspective. They don't take any consideration what the impact of their actions are on the other side. They don't look fully upon whatever is going on the other side. If it's not them, it's a plane-casting thing. In a long term, factors for effective long-term performance, they need to be able to see from the other perspectives of this one point.

Participant 2, a male leader, considered performance and effective working relationship as effects of networking and relationship building of the contractors with the government agencies. Participant 2 described contracting business as "nothing more than a collection of people." He believed, "if you're not able to network and develop those relationships, not only within the organization, but external relationships, then you're not going to be able to move forward."

Emotional intelligence of project managers. Six participants, 29% (see Table 2), also identified this sub-theme as a strategy for positive performance ratings. Participant 12, a female leader, considered emotional intelligence a necessary leadership quality a leader must possess. Participant 12 compared the relevance of emotional intelligence and having Ph.D. degree. She said, "The Ph.D. makes a difference and opens the doors and doing high-quality work makes a difference, but I think the emotional intelligence (EI) is such an important piece of doing good work. Participant 12 explained that EI is a requirement in dealing with client. She cited an example:

> … just in terms of consultation skills and working with a client, being able to read them, being able to ask questions in a way that they

feel safe enough answering, so I can really get to the bottom of what the issues are, developing relationships, sometimes pairing with internal people to consult, and able to not compete, but appreciate the differences and work together. I think a lot of it is emotional intelligence stuff.

Participant 17, a male leader, implicated the relevance of the leaders' ability to relate with his or her staff as well as with the clients. Participant 17 said, "It's the ability to relate personally with people to be successful, and that, it's mostly your employees, as well as the government people on the other side." Participant 17 shared that success for him is, "spend[ing] time talking to these people about things that are important to them as well as the government, the actual contract issues."

Participant 17 associated inter-personal skills with emotional intelligence. He said contractors may need to "learn to interface and communicate with these people on a human being to human being level." He believed an emotional intelligent leader understands the psychological and emotional concerns of leaders involved in the contracting projects.

Business insights of leaders. Participant 13, a male leader, cited that leaders in the contracting business must have foresight of the possible needs of the clients. He said,

> You must have obvious insight into what needs of the customer are, so you have an understanding of what the customer needs are, how to meet those needs, and how to effectively translate what they are asking for in an RFP [request for proposal] or specification or capabilities design document, and translate that into what truly is the desired outcome.

Participant 13 shared that clients may be unable to articulate the specifics of the works. He said the leader must be able to understand and define these needs. Participant 13 further explained,

> Everybody's perception of a good chocolate chip cookie is different, so you need to understand what it is that the customer's really, truly after. If the Navy, they might say their version of a chocolate chip cookie is Chips

Ahoy chocolate chip cookie, whereas the Army Special Operations Command might be something that's like hot, gooey, right out of the oven. You need to have an insight into what it takes to make and meet those customer expectations to make a valuable product, because the responsibility, it goes beyond just making a product.

In the words of Participant 20, leaders who have business insights are visionary leaders. Participant 20 considered visions as essential blueprint business plan of organizations that intend to engage in government projects. Participant 20 said,

I think that there are two leadership factors that are very important. Actually there are two more when I think about it. The first one is vision. When you own a business or you lead a business, you need to have a vision of the services that you're going to provide.

Business insights also mean the competency of leaders concerning the required work, working arrangement, and financial benefits out of the contract without sacrificing the quality of work. Participant 5, a male leader, described business insights to be valuable in the sustainability of firms engaged in government contracts. He said,

> One is, you have to have a clear understanding of the work to be done. That means for both the government and the contractor – the business … The second piece is … understanding what the contract compliance requirements are. Last but not least … is the budget controls. Everybody complains about the bleeding out of a contract. Nine times out of 10, either somebody asks for something that wasn't planned. In a lot of cases, you're contracting us or they're contracting us and not even know it. You end up having to clean this up at the back end. Those are the main areas that I think are … A good leader, on the business side, understands these challenges and then ensures that they're being met.

Good understanding of the bureaucracy. Six of the participants or 29% (see Table 2) claimed that the government scheme had unique systems of engagement that required flexibility, compliance, competency, and interpersonal skills from the leaders. Participant 3, a male leader, shared that contracting organizations must be flexible to adapt with the changes in the policies and services that may be required from them. He said, "A business owner needs to get a fine tune or adjust our services to meet the demands and/or actually get ahead of the demand that's coming." Participant 9, a male leader, also shared that in addition to leadership skills, the organization must have a leader "that has worked in the federal government and understands government contracts."

In understanding the bureaucratic system of government, leaders may need to acquire relevant experiences with these agencies. Participant 20, a female leader, believed experiences are essential in operationally implementing the government contracts. Participant 20 described that a visionary leader may not be enough to be successful in the contracting business environment. She explained, "There are people who have great vision, but they can't figure out how to implement or bring to reality the vision that they have. That operational aspect is very important, and I think they go hand in hand." Participant 8, a female leader, also supported this claim by stating, "Having someone on the team not only with the leadership skill sets and business skill sets, but someone that has worked in the federal government and understands government contracts."

Continuous organizational improvement. Participant 2, a male leader, implicated the organizational success to the ability of leaders to sustain organizational improvement. He believed competition with other contractors required professional standard and continuous education. Participant 2 articulated that flexibility of the changes requires leaders to upgrade knowledge and skills continuously to compete with other contractors. He said,

> You have to continuously renew your education, particularly in government because, well, it changes… it fluctuates, legislations change, procurement rules change, administrations change, directors change, Congress says we're not going to fund a particular program, that has a ripple effect. You have to be continuously renewing yourself, and informing those below you, or those that follow you the same way. You have to have training.

Participant 9, a male leader, figuratively described continuous improvement as the willingness of the leader to "stay[ing] hungry and being able to, or really excited about new opportunities and willing to take risks." He shared that "complacency or getting comfortable in a current position is not a contributor to future success." Participant 9 shared the organizational mission in relation to sustaining organizational improvement. Participant 9 said,

> We always have to be striving to do more and do better, deliver better on the contracts that we actually have, winning more contracts that might be outside our geographic or technical scope. We always have to be pushing forward for new experiences.

Accountability of actions and commitment. Leaders who had long-term and continuous positive performance ratings on projects with the government demonstrated accountability with their past and present engagements. Participant 20, a female leader, shared that there are leaders who initially demonstrated their commitment to comply with the project deliverables, but were unable to comply with the project provisions such as time and quality of the services rendered. Participant 20 described that as "… a successful leader, you must be accountable, not only for yourself as the CEO, but for your team and your company and the people who perform for your company." Participant 21, a male leader, reiterated the value of accountability by stressing the ability of the leaders to operationalize contract plans and activities through a willingness to work beyond extended hours. Participant 21 said,

> I think in addition to those two factors, the integrity, and the confidence is the drive. The leader … or the business owner has to have the drive that you have to put in the grind. You have to put in the hours; you have to put in the work in order to be successful. For long-term success, you have to see it. Part of the vision is how to sustain that over time. You need to be willing to grind and put in the work that it takes to get to the point of being a true, successful entrepreneur doing business with the federal government.

Integrity of the organization. Participant 21, a male business leader in contracting environment, shared that the integrity of the leader and the organization would yield trust and confidence from the "federal government as we're pursuing federal contracts." Participant 21 claimed,

> Integrity is the foundation. ... it builds your character and it allows clients and other contractors and peers to want to work with you based on who you are and the likability of knowing that you're going to do the right thing always. It's easy to get influenced, especially when you have great opportunities that you may not have had before, staring you in your face. Having that integrity is the background or the backbone of being of a great leadership factor.

Integrity for Participant 4, a male leader is "Being straightforward with either the COTR or contract officer when there is an issue. Not trying to hide if there is a problem."

Organizational competitiveness. Participant 21, a male leader, utilized the word "confidence" to associate the ability of leaders to compete during the procurement process. Participant 21 explained competition was evident among small and large businesses that aspired to win government contracts. He said, "They have may have the financial capacity or the human capital or the bonding, per se. As such, it can be daunting or intimidating if you will."

Participant 9, a male leader, added the leader must understand the "competitive environment." Participant 9 explained that several like-minded institutions were:

> ... seeking understanding that you might be going after similar opportunities, what their strengths and weaknesses might be, the kind of angles that they would be taking on a particular opportunity, and also how those competitors align with our understanding of the client. It's kind of a subset of the understanding of the customer, which is the competitive environment, going after that work.

This sub-theme contradicts the perspectives of other contractors who claimed as long as they demonstrated their perseverance, winning government contracts are relatively possible. The contradictions reflected in the experiences of the participants in this research study support the contentions of Brown (2011) who stated most government outsourcing lacked systemized accountability. Decisions of contractual agreements in the federal government indicated procurement practices of several officials are based on subjective indicators of quality services. This procurement practices could yield significant political issues in general, but particularly in government services (Witesman & Fernandez, 2013).

Available mentors of organizational leaders. Participant 14, a male leader, associated professionally prepared contractors with the availability of mentors. He believed that mentoring "…groom…successful contractors and successful bidder." Participant 14 claimed that mentors "will really help your leadership."

Theme 2: Behavioral or Trait-Based Attributes of Leaders

Theme 2 emerged from the aggregation of eight sub-themes (see Table 3), which refers to behavioral or trait-based leadership affecting positive government contractor performance. These sub-themes included: (a) collaborative leadership, (b) empowering and guiding others, (c) building relationship and trust, (d) driving for results, (e) care for others, (f) integrity, (g) decision-making competency, and (h) emotional intelligence. Each theme was presented and substantiated in this section.

Table 2 - Behavioral or Trait-Based Attributes of Leaders

Sub-Themes	Occurrences (number)	Occurrences (percentage)
Collaborative leadership	9	43
Empowering and guiding others	7	33
Building relationship and trust	6	29
Emotional intelligence	6	29
Driving for results	4	19
Care for others	4	19

Sub-Themes	Occurrences (number)	Occurrences (percentage)
Integrity	4	19
Decision-making competency	2	10

Collaborative leadership. This leadership behavior stressed the importance of teamwork in the organization. Nine, or 43% (see Table 3), of participants mentioned this sub-theme. Participant 8, a female leader, described collaboration as "cohesive leadership working together … toward accomplishing [our] goals and setting goals." She stressed the team could work together with shared goals. Participant 8 explained, "I think goal setting is critical to the growth, especially when small businesses start getting close to becoming other than small." Participant 6, a female participant, used the term "people skills" to implicate the ability of a leader to work along with the members of the team. Participant 6 described this behavior as follows:

> You have to be focused on people to be successful in this business. Whether it is talking with potential teaming partners, whether it's meeting and greeting government officials

to answer the point of hiring staff either for your corporate office or hiring staff that's going to be working for your company on a contract within the federal government. If you cannot reflect the comfort of having people skills as the leader of your company, your success rate gets questionable at some point in time.

This people skill was supported in the work of Plane and Green (2012) and Grudinschi et al. (2014) who implicated the importance of collaboration and partnerships in public service procurement. These studies claimed organizational significance for contractors and government agencies emanates from their collaborative partnership whereby government officials actively communicated their service specifications and needs.

Participant 9, a male leader, shared that collaboration had been a challenge for his leadership. He saw the importance of collaboration in "increasing the efficiency of the processes that we have so that things are done faster and better." Participant 9 further explained the expertise of individual members is crucial in the successful performance of any contract endeavors. He said,

The technical approaches that we bring to the table, specifically the design of the project that we bring on top of what USAID or what state would have, how we use the consultant, that's how we really try to bring our own style to the opportunities and that way distinguish ourselves.

Empowering and guiding others. In addition to collaboration, a successful leader in government contracting who collaborates with members of the team incorporate empowerment and guidance in leading the employees. Participant 5, a male business leader, shared that employees perform their responsibilities when they are empowered and properly guided. He explained, "They have to understand that you can delegate tasks you can delegate authority to do something, but you cannot delegate responsibility." When empowering employees, the leader could easily offer clear guidance "as to what it is that needs to be done on every single government contract that you're performing on." Participant 5 further stressed leaders may need to "ensure that they understand that relationship associated with responsibility."

Participant 4, a male business leader, implicated the need for the leaders to empower employees in solving relevant project issues. He shared that their organization recognizes the knowledge and skills of every employee and provides employees the opportunity to contribute and participate in accomplishing tasks as well as in resolving issues. Participant 4 said they ensured "we cover issues that each others are having to see if someone else has experienced that so we can do lessons learned, as well as try to build a team within the managers."

These findings relate to the ability of leaders to establish robust personal affiliations both internal and external the company by operating collaboratively with others (Mittal & Dorfman, 2012). Strengthening of working relationship with the stakeholders requires the leader to mentor and guide employees who are in charge of completing the contract projects (Robertson & Barling, 2013). This leadership characteristic aligns closely with elements of transformational leadership.

Building relationship and trust. According to six participants, or 29% (see Table 3), in the study, trust is built from an effective working relationship. Participant 9, a male leader, implicated client-based organizations had leaders who valued positive working environment with the contracting parties. He said leaders gained positive working relationship when clients trusted them. He said, "[leaders should] work to develop and cultivate trusting working relationships with people within the customer organizations." He further shared,

> We try to deliver to our product but also connect with our clients to understand what their needs are and make sure that what we are delivering is what they need. Over time, this builds a trust-based relationship, which helps to navigate when inevitable bumps come up.

Participant 12, a female leader, implicated that a leader who builds positive working relationship and provides positive feedback is beneficial in their work. She explained,

> The building relationships is key, not just for managing the contracts, but for doing good work where people want you to come back because they trust you and I can answer your

questions, and they're more open because especially in organization development work, you really need that from your client.

Participant 9, a male leader, stressed the relationship between trust, respect, and positive working relationship. He explained when there is trust and respect, employees working along with leaders strived to pursue the vision of the organization and delivered expected responsibilities. Participant 9 said, "We differentiate ourselves from the field with [that] not settling for good enough in delivery."

Participant 9, a male leader, stressed that "good working relationships with our client representatives over a long period of time" is an indication of the performance of the organization and the effective qualities of a leader. He said, " … a strong professional working relationship … helps to address challenges from a position of mutual trust and respect, rather than firefighting in crisis management."

Emotional intelligence. A participant identified "the capacity of the [leader] to be aware of, control, and express one's emotions, and to handle interpersonal relationships judiciously and empathetically." Participant

20, a female leader, stressed emotional maturity of leaders is essential in the management of people who may have a limited understanding of the project, including the challenges the leaders take in managing individual differences. She said an emotionally intelligent leader handles competently those employees who are uncaring, struggling, and emotionally incompetent in an adult-like organization.

Driving for results. Only four, or 19%, (see Table 3) of the participants identified the results-oriented leadership behavior. Participant 12, a female leader, considered "results-focused" characteristic of leader who remain engaged in the contract business. For her, "bigger companies" with several employees requires guidance to demonstrate "confident excellent work with high standards, and that's results-focused."

Care for others. Four or 19% (see Table 3) of the participant emphasized the importance of value-based leadership particularly the leader's care for his or her subordinates. Participant 18, a female leader, considered "genuine care and concern" for employees as an essential characteristic. She shared empathy for others motivated the employees to work with the leaders. Participant 8, also a female leader, considered "caring about your employees," which influenced their performance, thereby facilitating success. Participant 8 explained employee retention and positive performance were results of the leaders' ability to demonstrate care and empathy. She shared the experiences of her company:

> In the case of this company, we have two all hands meetings with our employees to bring them together and also to know about the company, the leadership, where the business is and where we're going in the future, and how they can be engaged to help in our growth.

Integrity. Four, or 19%, (see Table 3) of the participants shared the importance of integrity of the leader. Participant 18, a female leader, said, "I think the primary one is integrity and honesty." She explained, "If you do not have integrity, do not have honesty, whatever else you do, it's not going to work." Participant 18 associated integrity with trust, loyalty, and positive relationship with the client and subordinates.

Participant 7, a male leader, shared his views about honesty and positive performance from the organization. He said an honest leader reduces employees' fear, which gives them more time and opportunity to contribute to the organization. Participant 7 demonstrated this scenario by stating,

> ...to be honest with people, let them know exactly where you are, what the expectations are, to be clear. One of the other behaviors is to make sure that you control the organizational stress by allowing them to do the things that they need to do to get the job done and not have to worry about whether they're going to get paid or whether their vacations are going to come, but make sure all those things are taken care of so they can then function on the mission at hand of giving the best possible things, not things, but the best possible effort into accomplishing the goal of transcribing Veterans medical reports.

Decision-making competency. Making decisions is a primary role of every leader. Two, or 10% (see Table 3), of participants communicated this sentiment. Participant 2, a male leader, emphasized that "decisiveness" of the leader is essential in the delivery of efficient output. He explained, "People get hung up on not making decisions and it causes a backlog, a jam, or it causes procurement failures or performance failures." Participant 2 stressed that decisiveness demonstrated the ability of leaders to influence others and achieve accountabilities.

Participant 3, a male leader, indicated decisiveness to risk-taking. Participant 3 shared that inherent in running a business is the associated risk any leader should take. Participant 3, a male leader, shared that while risk "start[s] to multiply thereafter… a leader still has to move the company forward and to teach folks how to get through those situations that may go not in their favor." Participant 3 further described that leaders must "understand[ing] how to get to your win and having better averages, rather than going after the shotgun approach that many people would do, so more focused marketing and sales."

Theme 3: Understanding Bureaucratic Dynamics and Contract Requirements

Two of the themes in this study identified positive relationships with the client as an essential leadership attributes contractors have to build and maintain to yield positive performance ratings consistently in the government contracting business. In building positive relationship with the contracting professionals, the participants identified that leaders in the contracting business had to demonstrate abilities to comply all contract provisions as well as those unwritten request from the contracting government officials (see Table 4).

Table 3 - Understanding Bureaucratic Dynamics and Contract Requirements

Sub-Themes	Occurrences (number)	Occurrences (percentage)
Communication	16	76
Understanding bureaucratic dynamics	12	57
Positive relationship and trust	10	48
Fulfillment of contract provisions	10	48

Communication. Bureaucracies are shown in the pattern of communication that government officials adapted. Sixteen, or 76%, of the participants believed communication bridges the information gap between two or more agency officials. According to Participant 12, a female leader, contractors struggle to deliver quality products and services because contracting officials are "lazy about communicating clearly about what they want, so you respond to the RFP, and you often find out that what they want is quite different from the RFP." Participant 9 added that communication is a major issue in the government procurement process – particularly during proposal evaluation. He said, while the contracting officials provide "feedback on the proposals that we submit … we sometimes wonder how much is really genuine feedback." Participant 9 further added, "The feedback we get back is sometimes contradictory within itself or it's not very clear or very helpful." Participant 9 stressed that government procurement process conveyed evaluation results sometimes difficult to understand. He said, "It feels like there's more going on than just what the letter, the word on the page. That makes it harder for us to understand the client."

Participant 5 explained constant communication is essential in understanding the needs of the client. However, frequent communication with the contracting officials may have a negative side. He said these officials may get "… comfortable with your contractor and they'll make changes." Participant 5 shared additional tasking may need to be accommodated, but "… we need permission to do that from the contracting officer." He implicated this relationship only demonstrates the control of the contracting agency.

Participant 14, a male leader, supported the claims of other participants that establishment of effective communication and positive working relationship are related. He said unsatisfied clients are less communicative of their needs and wants. Participant 14 shared that to minimize bad reputations, his company ensured they establish communication and respectful relationship with government officials. Participant 14 said, "You must have that relationship, understanding, or respect between each other to have a successful project."

Understanding bureaucratic dynamics.
Twelve, or 57% (see Table 4), of the participants in this study described their contract performance as successful because they had in-depth knowledge of the government system. Participant 1, a male participant, described the relationship of the contractor and government agencies. He said, "The buyer has all the power. The seller has less power. Sets all the rules. Sets all the timelines." Participant 1 further shared the government agencies imposed their rules and the responsibilities of the contractors are to comply whatever and whenever order the contracting officials order or

instruct. In further describing the relationship between the contractor and the government, Participant 1 said, "The contractor becomes out of the second class citizen." He described that when contractors do not win bids on contracts, the government officials refuse to provide debriefings to unsuccessful offorers even though debreifings are required when requested timely and in accordance with FAR.

Participant 11, a male leader, described the bureaucratic system that government contracting companies have to understand. He shared there is a thin line difference between government service and commercial needs of the contractors with the government agencies. He said, "It may be a little be different but, there's a significant sensitivity about what is 'inherently governmental' can only be performed by a government civilian, and then what's the basic commercial in nature." Participant 11 implicated this type of working relationship impedes the "contractors' ability to provide its sound advice and input to work products."

Contractors are resources often dependent on the government for clarification, which affects their overall performance. Participant 11 described, "It's hard to give the government sage advice if you're only being given half of the story and you're trying to produce a coherent and cogent product for them."

Positive relationship and trust. Ten, or 48%
(see Table 4), of the participants implicated the
government procurement process is favorable to
government contracting companies with which they have
established positive relationships and trust. Participant
14, a male leader, understands that in addition to the
expertise and service pricing, almost all government
agencies would want to award projects to contractors
whom they had positive work experiences and trust. He
believed that just like his leadership direction, the
government would wish to procure service from sellers
who valued the integrity of their work. He said, "I tend to
try to do business with people I know and trust, as far as
commercial or government, because at the end of the
day you guys are going to spend a lot of time together."

Participant 5, a male leader, explained that
relationship and trust are unwritten criteria in the
selection of project contractors. He said,

> The stronger your relationship between the
> contractor and the government … the clear[er]
> understanding of roles and responsibilities,
> clear[er] understanding of what it is that you're

trying to achieve, clear[er] understanding of what it's going to take to achieve that, either through work planning or some other form of planning.

Participant 21, a male leader, stressed trust is "the most important relationships … made from both a tangible and intangible position." Participant 21 explained the binding agreement between two parties necessitate the need for trustful exchanges to fulfill binding accountabilities. He justified that "There's a trust that goes on between the two that understood." Participant 2, a male leader, described government contracting as a "marriage." He said, "If there's not trust in that marriage, it's going to manifest itself in the performance. Lack of trust, lack of communication, personality clashes, the government being overbearing or trying to force the contractor to do certain things."

Trust was also mentioned by Participant 13 (a male leader), as the foundation of a strong, positive working relationship. Participant 13 shared there are small contractors who passed the initial qualification screening, but are unable to deliver quality products and services. Participant 13 shared government officials acquire / procure contract services from contractors to whom they entrust their careers. He said, "I'm not going to choose you as my contractor because you have a perceived risk and it could impact my career." He further explained,

> Government acquisition officers and program managers quite often select companies based on how they think that that company could impact their career, and not on the product itself, and they don't care about the end result or what gets the best stewardship for the taxpayers' money or anything else.

Fulfillment of contract provisions. Ten, or 48% (see Table 4), of the participants implicated the contractors must have the institutional knowledge and experiences in fulfilling the provisions of the contract works. Participant 14 shared that this is the reason for the government procurement officials to select organizations with owner(s) or business partner(s) who were previously employed in the government agencies as a government services (GS) worker. Participant 14 claimed that training contractor staff or groups of experts who would fulfill specific functions in the government is timely and costly for the government. Government procurement ensured that – with limited resources – contractors can deliver the required services. Participant 14 believed contractors must "meet the contractual requirement … you are not supposed to go beyond that. You are not supposed to go less than that."

Five of the participants shared that positive contract performance is largely dependent on the ability of the contractors to maintain legal boundaries between the contractors and government employees. Participant 17 stressed government contractor employees are not the same as government employees and are not able to directly utilize government resources and access the non-public information. Participant 14 shared,

> I've seen some people try and deliver above and beyond what's in the contract by saying, "We want to deliver more. We want to do better," but that will only get you in trouble. You just have to understand the industry you are in. In government, we are not (a group of) Silicon Valley, free-wheeling people … just out there. We are not research and school. We are very strict. That contract is very clear.

Two of the participants identified that shared goals can influence a positive working relationship between a contractor and government agency, and implicated their desire to complete the project requirements in federal government agencies not aligned with their organizational goals and objectives. Participant 16, a female leader, shared,

We have a government employee right now who is the type of person who is never satisfied and my goal is for him to finish the work with us. No more than that. Just that we'll actually be able to finish and get paid for the work. Other government employees we actually enjoy working for and have shared values looking at the work as something that we're doing collaboratively. So, the type of government employee that's accepting the work is critical to the style of reporting of company success.

Theme 4: Resource-Based Capacity as an Impediment

The fourth theme emerged from the need of the contractors to fulfill all available resources for use during the completion of the contract work. The participants enumerated human, monetary, raw materials, and other relevant capital necessary in winning a government contract projects. Participant 6, a female leader, articulated human resources as "people skills." Participant 8, also a female leader, reflected skills and knowledge of the government staff behind the contract work are invaluable to contractors. Participant 8 enumerated knowledge and experiences in "in the federal government and understands government contracts."

Financial resources are budget funding used by managers to pay goods and services for the production of services. All participants agree financial resources are an essential requirement during the procurement process. Participant 20, a female leader, shared that the government is interested in evaluating the project proposals and how the organization would fund the project activities. Participant 20 differentiated the large and small business contractors according to their overhead cost and the relevant project pricing quoted during the request for proposals. Participant 20 shared, "Small businesses are sometimes considered to be cheaper than big businesses. We're not going to pay you as much because you're small. The larger companies may have larger overhead, bigger office space."

Raw materials are the elements used directly to deliver service products. Participant 21, a male leader, enumerated "equipment, materials, or supplies" necessary for use of the people working under contract. Participant 1, a male leader, stressed "time and materials (T&M)" as essentials in the completion of the project. Participant 1 noted these factors should be enumerated in the project proposal. Participant 1 considered this as "huge expenses … that is critical for us to be able to do that work."

Other relevant capital essential in the delivery of a quality and efficient product includes agency intelligence, competitive intelligence, and bidding strategies. These capital are intangible and requires the social and emotional intelligence of the leaders in small contracting organizations. Participant 14, a male leader, considered available "mentors" as a resource that can be used during the competitive bidding process. Participant 14 said mentors could help the leaders in the preparation of project proposals. Mentors can be personnel or leaders within the government procurement panel who can help groom the leader and the company.

Capitalization to finance quality work. All 21 participants (100% in the study) perceived government procurement officials have strong biases in awarding large and complicated projects to large contracting companies that can afford to hire competent staff and finance expensive materials. Participant 20, a female leader, said, "There is an unspoken, sometimes spoken preference for larger businesses" in awarding government projects. Participant 20 shared the common misconception concerning "Small business, sometimes the perceived "S" for small equals 'stupid'." She further stressed that – to the contrary – less prioritized and limited budget projects were awarded to small business contractors. Participant 20 shared the common responses of the government when asked about their project rejection. Participant 20 said, "Small businesses are sometimes considered to be cheaper than big businesses. We're not going to pay you as much because you're small. The larger companies may have larger overhead, bigger office space."

While the organization of SBA was to ensure that organizations with limited financial resources are given equal opportunities to participate in the government bidding process, Participant 21, a male leader, believed small organizations still have to prove their sources of funds to justify their capabilities to undertake the government service. Participant 21 said that small business contractors were serious in attending project biddings should initiate fund sourcing to support the resources needed for the production of the service contracts. Participant 21 used the term "bonding" or service bond required when awarded with a project. Participant 21 said, "You will not be able to perform on most construction projects without it [bond]." According to Participant 21, SBA offers assistance to small businesses in the use of lending institutions that can provide basic funding requirement or bonds of the project. Participant 21 explained,

> ... financial institutions ... that provide loans and lines of credit that will allow small businesses to be able to manage the operations or start the operations. Build the operations. By having the cash flow or the capital necessary to sustain while the

government is paying within a net fourteen or net thirty or sometimes even later. It gives them the ability to perform.

Participant 3, a male leader, stressed the importance of financial capital of the organization to sustain the operation of the business with consideration of the potential delays of the service payment from the government agency. Participant 3 said, on behalf of the business leaders, they "… need to understand they need to have at least a quarter's worth, if not two quarter's worth of dollars for all the employees that they're going to have, and not be weary of that cash flow." Participant 3 considered the contracting company employees an asset of the organization and that losing these valuable assets would mean losing opportunities to acquire future projects.

Theme 5. Competitive Intelligence as a Valuable Resource

All participants in the study articulated an intangible, but very relevant resource of the organization crucial in winning a project. These participants enumerated these intangible assets as knowledge of the working environment and requirement, bureaucracy, system, and working dynamics necessary to succeed in highly volatile work services. Eight of the participants verbatim identified the veteran or retired personnel who started their own contracting business after their government service were at the advantage of having a competitive edge over other contractors. In fact, Participant 4 mentioned the 2010 GAO decertification order to eliminate certifications of "fraudulent small disabled vet-owned businesses, and veteran-owned small businesses within the system." Participant 4 shared there are legitimate veteran-owned businesses that demonstrated their competency to bid and deliver services to the government. Participant 4 explained that accusations came from the bidding competitions, which projects are mostly awarded to veteran-owned businesses. Participant 4 shared the experience.

> They were holding subcommittee hearing with
> the small business and the VA [U.S.
> Department of Veterans Affairs]. Vet Force, at
> the time I was on the board, was invited to talk
> to that very issue. Vet Force invited me to talk
> to the subcommittee, because we had actually
> submitted a bid [that] that very situation
> occurred.

Knowledge of the industry through experience. Sixteen, or 76% (see Table 5), of the participants reiterated the importance of working experiences, either as a former government employee or as working professional from large government contractors. Participant 10, a male leader, considered knowledge of the industry an asset when hiring contracting company employees. He said while there are tangible resources that could be enumerated when identifying essential resources for successful business, work experience in the industry would help employees and potential leaders understand the dynamics and the unspoken yet required works to complete and satisfy the procurement officers. Participant 10 shared how these intangible resources can be acquired.

> I think a good way to start is to work for a large firm and be successful at that firm and work for a successful firm. It can be any firm that's successful in government contracting, and gain the experience under the tutelage or what have you, under the training of someone that's already been successful doing that. Whether it's a global firm or whatever firm, to learn it.

Table 4 - Competitive Intelligence as a Valuable Resource

Sub-Themes	Occurrences (number)	Occurrences (percentage)
Knowledge of the industry through experience	16	76
Network	13	62

Participant 11, a male leader, reiterated how veteran-owned businesses successfully acquire and complete small or large government contracts. Participant 11 equated "knowledge of the industry" with "network." Participant 11 explained, "I think for a small business, you're only as good as your network." Participant 11 further explained, "If you don't have military experience, it's the people you've found through the years that you end up doing business with. That includes your client base and the ones you've worked on site with." He termed this asset as "intelligence on opportunities that are coming out." Leaders are using this intelligence in hiring employees, making inquiries of bidding requirement, and implementing effective strategies to win the bid projects.

Participant 15, a female leader, supported this contention by stressing the importance of "mentoring." She said while formal training is essential, successes in this type of business "rely on large businesses or more experienced businesses, colleague to colleague, learn as you go training on this." She further claimed knowledge of the industry comes from "a formal or informal mentor protégé relationship with a more experienced firm." She believed "most small businesses learn from another business."

Participant 19, a male leader, also identified the mentor-protégé program as an essential opportunity Small Business Administration (SBA) leaders have invested in "to have larger experienced contractors partner up and mentor a small, inexperienced protégé company." Participant 19 further claimed small and large contractors' relationship are equally beneficial as small organizations will have the opportunity to learn and earn from the partnership while large organizations will earn more credentials in the government contracting services.

Network. Thirteen, or 62% (see Table 5), of the participants identified networking as a valuable competitive intelligence. Participant 11, a male leader, said for "small business, you're only as good as your network ... networking is the key." Participant 13 also agreed, "Networking is pretty much the only thing that works." Participant 13 shared how a government procurement process show biases to an established network of contractors. He shared a verbatim statement from the procurement officer, "Our goal is to get [you] companies out here talking to each other and networking so that you can come together as a team to offer us a better product." Participant 13 further added establishing a network would need insightful and personal relationship with the customer.

Participant 16, a female leader, described competitive intelligence as the ability of the organization to utilize existing networks to learn, partner, and experience the government contract service. Participant 16 believed leaders who valued effective strategies resorted to identifying trusted partners. "They're also very difficult to find because the atmosphere is so competitive." She explained competition emerged in the industry because of "government funding cutback, which becomes more difficult for companies to sustain their own workforce and help other companies." Participant 16 stressed to have a competitive edge; leaders need "networking and confidence have to come across to be seen by another company or the government."

Applications to Professional Practice

This research study contributes to the understanding of the nature of the relationship between the government and the contractor and the government contractor's employees. The desire to treat the contractor as part of the team is understandable; government employees must realize the potential risks they expose on the government and contractor if they allow special treatment. The small business community's improvement in contract performance may occur through government leaders' and government contracting officers increased understanding of government contractor's business challenges. Results of this new understanding require movement toward initiatives to create objective and relevant performance standards (Binderkrantz et al., 2011). In this research study, the contractors requested collaboration, partnership, and communication to work more effectively while performing their contract deliverables and tasks. There are associated risks inherent in sharing the resources including exchanges of non-public information.

As two organizations collaborate to perform certain government tasks, organizational rules and regulations are expected to be applied. Government employees are subject to federal laws and regulations compliance, as well as any applicable government agencies' rules. Contractor personnel are employees of a contractor; they are subject to the laws that apply to all individuals the terms and conditions of their individual employment agreements with their employer and the applicable terms and conditions under and of their employer's contract with the government. Federal regulations and agency policies exist for the purpose of consistency; however, these regulations and policies are often confusing and conflicting to small businesses, while they allow for flexibility and deviation for government personnel. This research study articulates the relevance of the leadership strategies in contracting business with considerations of existing government agency bureaucracies and how leadership behaviors apply to situations that may arise within the government-contractor relationship. Also articulated is how impactful confusing, conflicting, and loosely applied regulations often are on the small business community.

The procurement practices rely on awarding service contracts to trained former government employees who possess in-depth knowledge of the government system. Contractor personnel may have been members of active duty military services or government service (GS) workers. This research study highlights the significant of former government employees who now serve as entrepreneurs and the influence they can present to procurement officials. The inherent ties of these individuals and business owners create a significant advantage to success in obtaining government contracting opportunities and exhibiting successful performance. The findings of the research unearthed variables of standard functionalities essential to creating sustainable solutions for government contractors and in public procurement through positive performance. The research findings support the need for continued education and research into the effects of long-term, business development, planning, and leadership practices to provide strategies for firms to implement. As the government adopts sustainable procurement programs, contracting officials gain the influence to stimulate copied behavior for other levels of government and other sectors (Grob & Benn, 2014). The study results provide strategies for implementation in aiding the success of small and women-owned small businesses, including the integration of strategies in support of successful business partnership practices between the federal government contracting acquisition agency and the small business contractor. The collection of information derived from the study offers effective methods for small businesses to practice when contemplating or in the early stages of the public procurement process.

To increase the range of contracts that incorporate performance, an essential element is to engage with existing and prospective contractors who practice incentivization to develop innovative solutions (Erridge & Hennigan, 2012). This research study has enhanced the body of knowledge in a burgeoning field of public procurement by researching strategies that increased the chances of sustained success for small business owners that conduct business with the federal government. The results of the study revealed both small business representatives and government officials need more training and access to procurement related laws and policies. There seems to be a disconnect between the training provided – both on the government and businesses' side – and what is practiced. The small business community feels government decision makers do not understand their deviations from policy and how the need to cultivate personal relationships affects their ability to participate and be successful in government contracting. The increased knowledge and information should amplify the understanding of the leadership strategies that exist, how to employ those enhanced strategies, and how these leadership knowledge and skill strategies impact contract performance ratings.

The literature review revealed a relationship between small business and leadership styles and a correlation of the two variables to organizational performance. The findings from this study may help leaders and managers of businesses in the government contracting community understand and employ contributing strategies for success. Successful strategies provide a baseline to aid small business leaders in increasing the level of service and positive communications provided to the government agency representative and contracting officer. An increased level of output may result in increasing the contracting companies' competitive advantage, improve the contracting companies' performance markers, and add a positive return on investment (ROI) to the sustainability of their business' strategic revenue goals within the industry. Understanding leadership strategies that allow government officials to become more compassionate to challenges, they can subsequently improve practice during contract performance, and can move to a win-win position and partnership between two parties during contract performance. This alignment of goals provides content and context to improve a small business leader's ability to communicate, comply, and provide government contracting officer's information required to assist them in making decisions in the best interest of the government on contract award.

Implications for Social Change

Since the inception of this research study, issues in the public procurement have been a challenge (Flynn & Davis, 2014). In this study, the researcher has documented essential leadership factors affecting the success of small business contracting companies, as well as the leadership attributes necessary in providing positive ratings during performance and deliverables of government contracts. A noteworthy contribution of this study was that leadership attributes in the small business administration require a combination of trait-based, value-based, and outcome-based leadership. These leadership attributes offer positive insights to improving contracting performance. Communication was identified as a contributing factor in the success of the small government contracting business. This meant leaders should strategically align company goals with the policies internally and externally to their government contracting company organization to communicate with various leaders of the agency the company support concerning relevant specifications of the government projects.

The discovery of leadership and management communications solutions based on the findings of this research study contribute to the literature and research on the deficiency of resources for small business sustainability in government contracting. In industrialized nations, public procurement accounts for a substantial share of gross domestic product that makes it imperative to economic development for the government to utilize this potential (Preuss, 2011). The identification of leadership and communications mechanisms that bridge the gap in each entity's understanding and representation offers the opportunity to add value to local economies through employment creation. Small businesses retain a great deal of responsibility in the economy as the technological lead in the global marketplace resulting in one-third of all new patents issued (Cronin-Gilmore, 2012). The research study's participants provided insight to help make sense of the government contract, past-performance, rating process and provide recommendations for small businesses to successfully navigate that process. The results should encourage business owners that fall within the research study's identified socio-economic groups, with access to federal set-asides, to increase their competition for federal government contracts. Minority-owned, women-owned, and veteran-owned firms comprise examples of minority representation of government contractors, and may benefit from the implementation of identified strategies that predict future success.

As highlighted in the study, the American economy continues to rely on the employment opportunities offered through small business participation (Cronin-Gilmore, 2012). The identification of best-practice leadership strategies that contribute to successful performance outcomes of some small businesses in federal contracts provides a perspective for aspiring or struggling companies to increase contract performance and may assist in the proliferation of participation in contracting opportunities. Findings may also encourage Historically Underutilized Business (HUB), Service Disabled Veteran Owned Small Business (SDOSB), and Woman Owned Small Businesses (WOSB) just getting started and do not know where to begin, a reference point or roadmap for how to navigate the government procurement processes and knowledge of the resources that have helped previous companies succeed.

Recommendations for Action

The intent of this study was to provide lived experiences of small business leader's perception of the impact of leadership strategies in the performance of government procurement opportunities. The research study's results, conclusions, and recommendations can be used to expand further academic research to advance social change and leadership methodology, processes, procedures, communications, and positive interactions in the acquisition process of government contracting services. Through the understanding of the procurement practices – particularly leadership factors influencing the positive ratings success of government contracts – government leaders could take actions in harmonizing the system in a way that truly fosters a fair, competitive, objective, and outcome-based procurement process.

How to get government businesses to satisfy government agencies is not an objective process. While performance objectives are clearly stated in the contract, the bureaucratic environment dynamic indicates a need to cultivate government relationships, while excelling in performance.

This study offers viable evidence to leaders and managers who serve as strategic decision makers within their organizations and whom liaise with contracting officers within the federal government agencies. Small businesses may face severe disadvantages to doing business with the federal government without the protocol and understanding of processes within each agency. This research study identified different federal government agencies implemented the procurement process differently. The harmonization of the policies through the restructuring of procurement laws and regulations that negatively impact small business participation and performance could significantly guide leaders in the government to act with more congruency from agency to agency. The insight provided by the research study sample population of participants indicated the government procurement system may need to offer more training, assistance, and increase opportunities through decreasing outdated and irrelevant requirements that act as barriers to the small business community.

The resulting conclusion identified themes from coded responses that indicated it is critical for leaders to adapt leadership practices deemed appropriate for the situation. In this study, factors from different leadership theories emerged in the analysis.

The first theory that arose is leadership strategies that influence positive performance ratings. Leadership attitude, tenacity, work ethic and perseverence were terms used to describe strategies for succesful performance. Contracts in the government can last from months to years. When dealing with the government it is important to remember one is dealing with the largest beuracratic structure in the country. It is important that contractors demonstrate long-term, quality performance and an effective working relationship; therefore, effective management to the communication influences healthy working relationships. To be successful, it is important to deliver on contract requirements while continuing to foster relationships, regardless of how one may feel about fairness or accuracy in any rejections.

The second theory is small business leaders must empower their leaders and business developers. It is important for leaders of small businesses to build relationships with their customers (government agencies and representatives) and their (contract) employees. Government contractors may employ staff working in government sites in other states and often other countries. Ensuring employees continue to feel a part of the organization is important to the relationship built with the government customer. Employees represent their (employer) organization, which makes it important for their leadership to communicate, train, and help those contract employees help the company drive business and business development for better results. Understanding bureaucratic dynamics and contract requirements require education training and communication. Mentioned previously is the need for training for small business leaders that teaches policies, regulations, and how to communicate with government officials. The onus is on business leaders to empower themselves and understand the regulations governing the industry in which they perform. With the available resources identified by small business leaders who participated in this research study, coupled with impediments mentioned, further highlights the need of businesses to aggressively seek or create training and resources the small businesses need to be successful.

Lastly, competitive intelligence is a valuable resource. In-depth knowledge of the industry through years of experience is important. Some of the most successful companies are owned or led by former government employees who have navigated the processes and procedures of government contracting from the inside. These individuals have insight into the culture of the government and specifically the agencies in which they worked. They are able to bring their experience to the government contracting community to add value to external vendor (contracting) companies. Both business leaders and government entities such as the Small Business Administration (SBA) and the Department of Defense (DoD) recognizes organizations are only as good as their network. Business leaders and government officials do business with people they like. Fostering relationships with the Contracting Officer, Program Office representatives, and each agency's Office of Small & Disadvantaged Business Utilization (OSDBU) is a critical path to small business success. Teaming, partnering, and mentoring is perhaps the second most important protocol for small businesses. There are a number of mentor-protégé programs designed to help small businesses combine resources for growth. Some form of teaming, mentoring and partnering has become critical over the last decade in contracting to get access to contracts that allow for growth. The different leadership practices identified indicated the need for flexibility in practices to support the demands of the government agency clients while also complying with the project requirements and the potential to earn contracts in the future. Adaptability, both while performing on specific requirements, and how they operate as regulations, industries and key decision makers within the government change.

Public procurement positions, as a significant contributor to achieving sustainable development, continue to gain positive initiatives towards this evolution in other countries (Melissen & Reinders, 2012). History contributes to sustainable change by creating mechanisms for feedback available to employ variations of future organizational practices (Prywes, 2011). The research conclusions provided within this research study provides practitioners with a view of successful practices to employ within the government contracting acquisition and procurement field. Leaders and managers should recognize available practices: training, networking, relationship building, and staying abreast of industry changes for sustained success.

When entering the government contracting field small business leaders and managers should develop a strategic plan for to address capacity, resources, education, finances, building their network, marketing and relationship building to the government, competition, teaming partners, and a plan for growth. Strategic planning in government contracting is necessary. Planning must be adaptable as industries and trends change. Government contracting is not cut and dry, and is a uniquely dynamic field. Patience, adaptability, planning, and persistence from businesses leaders are important.

Recommendations for Further Research

The study explored perceived practices from the account of small business leaders. The foundation of the research arose from the gap in literature in the budding field of public procurement related to positive performance ratings on contract deliverables. The lack of available information on variables affecting performance and government contracts as they related to small business concerns created limitations for the qualitative discussion of current literature. As Bradshaw and Chang (2013) suggested, the government should standardize past performance databases and agree on quantifiable metrics to capture objective data. As Hiles (2015) highlighted, simply performing at high levels has not been enough to produce positive (past) performance ratings. Using competitive intelligence, cultivating relationships, understanding the bureaucratic environment of the agency, and finding ways to network and navigate are equally, if not more important, to views of successful performance, than actual contract delivery. Future research examining actual variables through a quantitative or mixed method correlation study measuring specific strategies and contract performance of small businesses could address this limitation. Exploratory sequential designs apply elements of qualitative and quantitative approaches in separate segments of the study that begin with the collection and analysis of qualitative data; the quantitative data (can) then build on the initial qualitative results (Stentz, Plano Clark, & Matkin 2012). A researcher may consider measuring specified strategies and actual ratings to determine how specific variables correlate to contract performance ratings.

Currently, evaluation is hampered by the lack of adequate tools for government officials to collect, analyze, and report relevant past performance information (Bradshaw & Su, 2013). Insight into past performance information from the federal government's perspective is under-represented (Hiles & Wells, 2015). Research that explores how government officials perceive or define positive contractor performance, and how those perceptions correlate to performance ratings may provide further insight into strategically available advancements of small business leaders. In the DC Metropolitan area, assistance is available from entities such as the SBA, the Procurement Technical Assistance Programs (PTAP), Small Business Development Centers (SBDC), Women's Business Center (WBC), and Veteran Business Outreach Centers (VBOC). Despite the dissemination of information from these resources, performance issues of small business persist. Future researchers may need to determine specific curriculum development of these specific programs, and how they can be tailored to foster improvement in contract performance. Findings from the study indicate the importance to knowledge of the bureaucratic process and policy and regulations that govern federal procurement, it is important small business representatives know and understand them.

Confusing and contradictory FAR policy and agency proceedures were mentioned as barriers for small businesses access to government contracting opportunities. Research into the specific policies and practices that make small business leaders hesitant about provding their services to the government can help the SBA and other entities that provide assistances to government contractors tailor training and resources to better assist the small businesses interested in obtaining government contracts.

The limitations included the restrictions on generalized data for all contracting opportunities or contract types. The population for this study consisted of small business leaders in the Washington DC metropolitan area. A larger scale exploratory study of the specific contract types and strategies that facilitate positive performance may further assist small companies that perform within specific industries. Sustainability implies long-term practices and measurements of performance. The current study omits consideration for any period for success measurement. Exploring successful practices over a significant period, a case study may capture a long-term perspective of strategic planning in small businesses.

Reflections

The research process has been a humbling and exciting experience. When embarking on this project the researcher felt overwhelmed because of the size and complexity of writing a doctoral level research project. As the researcher continued to immerse themselves in the literature, the experience turned into more of a journey.

The opportunity to meet and interview business leaders gave a greater understanding of their challenges. As a Contracting Officer for the federal government working in the DC area, this was the researcher's first experience seeing procurement from the perspective of small business owners. Many of these individuals worked around the clock and had some eye-opening feedback about the phenomenon. Echoed throughout the industry is the lack of understanding from government of how decisions influence small business.

The other sentiments of participants echoed seemed to be the lack of accountability of government officials. Agency deciding-officials' actions, based on personal motives, may mean the survival or detriment of a small government contracting business. There seemed to be a lack of accountability for improper or critical actions by contracting officers within federal government agencies, that could result in a small government contractor business failing.

The federal government agencies can facilitate more success of its small business contractors by improving regulations and offering more positive, professional, and ethical treatment of small businesses in the acquisition process. Through fostering relationships, positive networking, and increased communications, small business leaders can develop better ROI business development and leadership strategies for sustained success. The researcher's professional position has always been to constitute the practice of protecting the taxpayer, which meant being on the other side of the negotiation table with small business leaders. The semi-structured, open-ended interviews forced a connection with the interviewees as the researcher listened to their lived experiences. The researcher obtained insight into the small business government contractor representatives and leaders' trials and tribulations of striving for success in conducting business with the federal government.

Summary and Study Conclusions

Small business participation in growing businesses that create new jobs is essential to the recovery of the U.S. economy (e.g., Great Recession of 2008-2012). Understanding the significance of small business participation to the economy, the government increases funding flow to small businesses by making tax dollars available to them through government contracting opportunities. The government spends resources getting small businesses contracting dollars.

Agencies that advocate for small businesses, for example, the SBA, lack proven data for small business leaders to help them their companies be successful, once federal government agency contracts are obtained. To contribute to this deficiency in research and literature for small business leaders in the federal government contracting arena, the researcher explored strategies small business leaders use to achieve and increase positive performance ratings on government contracts. Information was obtained by interviewing 21 small business leaders who work for federal government contracting businesses located within 30 miles of Washington, DC, that additionally had favorable contract performance ratings on a minimum of three government contract vehicles.

Using thematic analysis, the researcher found behavioral, value-based, and trait-based leadership characteristics essential to leaders in managing government contracts with favorable contract performance ratings. The researcher identified that small government contracting businesses are an integral part of federal government procurement and acquisition activities. It may be difficult to distinguish between contractors and civil service employees for the service contract responsibilities attached for each entity. This qualitative descriptive research study enhances literature and research in the emerging field of effective procurement (Dimitri, 2013). The findings provide new information on leadership strategies available for implementation for small business leadership to increase success in government contract performance via increased positive performance ratings. This information fills gaps in leadership education, provides business leaders and managers with information from industry practitioners desiring to participate in government contracting opportunities, and contributes to the empirical literature on leadership and contract performance measurement. As a business topic in its infancy, it is anticipated that continued research would increase scholarly insight, and add to the body of knowledge for small businesses seeking success in the field of government contracting.

REFERENCES

Adams, R., & Funk, P. (2012). Beyond the glass ceiling: Does gender matter? *Management Science, 58,* 219-235. doi:10.1287/mnsc.1110.1452

Ageron, B., Gunasekaran, A., & Spalanzani, A. (2012). Sustainable supply management: An empirical study. *International Journal of Production Economics, 140,* 168-182. doi:10.1016/j.ijpe.2011.04.007

Alvesson, M., & Sandberg, J. (2011). Generating research questions through problematization. *Academy of Management Review, 36,* 247-271. doi:10.5465/AMR.2011.59330882

Ameer, R., & Othman, R. (2012). Sustainability practices and corporate financial performance: A study based on the top global corporations. *Journal of Business Ethics, 108,* 61-79. doi:10.1007/s10551-011-1063-y

Amirkhanyan, A. A. (2011). What is the effect of performance measurement on perceived accountability effectiveness in state and local government contracts? *Public Performance & Management Review, 35,* 303-339. doi:10.2753/PMR1530-9576350204

Ates, A., & Bititci, U. (2011). Change process: a key enabler for building resilient SMEs. *International Journal of Production Research, 49,* 5601-5618. doi:10.1080/00207543.2011.56382543.2011.563836

Avery, G. C., & Bergsteiner, H. (2011). Sustainable leadership practices for enhancing business resilience and performance. *Strategy & Leadership, 39*(3), 5-15. doi:10.1108/10878571111128766

Awortwi, N. (2012). Contracting out local government services to private agents: An analysis of contract design and service delivery performance in Ghana. *International Journal of Public Administration, 35,* 886-900. doi:10.1080/01900692.2012.686033

Bail, P. G., Jr. (2010). The demise of the federal government small business program. *Defense AR Journal, 17,* 77-92. Retrieved from http://www.dau.mil/publications/DefenseARJ/default.aspx

Bansal, P., & Corley, K. (2012). Publishing in AMJ - Part 7: What's different about qualitative research. *Academy of Management Journal, 55,* 509-513. doi:10.5465.amj.2012.4003

Binderkrantz, A. S., & Christensen, J. G. (2012). Agency performance and executive pay in government: An empirical test. *Journal of Public Administration Research & Theory, 22,* 31-54. doi:10.1093/jopart/mur039

Binderkrantz, A. S., Holm, M., & Korsager, K. (2011). Performance contracts and goal attainment in government agencies. *International Public Management Journal, 14,* 445-463.

doi:10.1080/10967494.2011.657116

Boiral, O., & Gendron, Y. (2011). Sustainable development and certification practices: Lessons learned and prospects. *Business Strategy and the Environment, 20*, 331-347. doi:10.1002/bse.701

Bradshaw, J., & Su, C. (2013). Past performance as an indicator of future performance: Selecting an industry partner to maximize the probability of program success. *Defense AR Journal, 20*, 59-80. Retrieved from http://www.dau.mil/publications/DefenseARJ/default.aspx

Brandon, D. M., Long, J. H., Loraas, T. M., Mueller-Phillips, J., & Vansant, B. (2014). Online instrument delivery and participant recruitment services: Emerging opportunities for behavioral accounting research. *Behavioral Research in Accounting, 26*, 1-23. doi:10.2308/bria-50651

Brown, A. (2014). The place of ethnographic methods in information systems research. *International Journal of Multiple Research Approaches, 8*, 166-178. doi:10.5172/mra.2014.8.2.166

Brown, A., & Iacono, J. (2012). Ethnographic research methods in business and information systems research. In *European Conference on Research Methodology for Business and Management Studies* (pp. 79). Kidmore End, United Kingdom: Academic Conferences International.

Brown, K. N. (2011). Government by contract and the structural constitution. *Notre Dame Law Review, 87*, 491. Retrieved from http://ndlawreview.org/

Bublak, D. R. (2014). Barriers to small business participation in federal overseas contracts and subcontracts. *Contract Management, 54*(5), 67-75. Retrieved from http://www.ncmahq.org

Chaturvedi, D., & Gautam, V. (2013). Performance contracting as an instrument for improving performance in government: An Indian experience. *International Journal of Public Administration, 36*, 408-425. doi:10.1080/01900692.2013.773028

Chenail, R. J. (2011). Interviewing the investigator: Strategies for addressing instrumentation and researcher bias concerns in qualitative research. *Qualitative Report, 16*, 255-262. Retrieved from http://www.nova.edu/ssss/QR/

Coletta, D. (2013). Principal-agent theory in complex operations. *Small Wars & Insurgencies, 24*, 306-321. doi:10.1080/09592318.2013.778016

Coenen, M., Stamm, T. A., Stucki, G., & Cieza, A. (2012). Individual interviews and focus groups in patients with rheumatoid arthritis: A comparison of two qualitative methods. *Quality Life Research, 21*, 359-370. doi:10.1007/s11136-011-9943-2

Cook, C. (2012). Email interviewing: generating data with a vulnerable population. *Journal of Advanced Nursing, 68*, 1330-1339. doi:10.1111/j.1365-2648.2011.05843.x

Cronin-Gilmore, J. (2012). Exploring marketing strategies in small businesses. *Journal of Marketing Development & Competitiveness, 6*, 96-107. Retrieved from http://www.na-businesspresss.com/

Decker, P., Durand, R., Mayfield, C. O., McCormack, C., Skinner, D., & Perdue, G. (2012). Predicting implementation failure in organization change. *Journal of Organizational Culture, Communications and*

Conflict, 16(2), 39-59. Retrieved from
http://www.alliedacademies.org/Public/Default.aspx

Dimitri, N. (2013). "Best value for money" in procurement. *Journal of Public Procurement, 13*, 149-175. Retrieved from
http://pracademics.com/index.php/jopp

Doh, J. P., & Quigley, N. R. (2014). Responsible leadership and stakeholder management: Influence pathways and organizational outcomes. *Academy of Management Perspectives, 28*, 255-274. doi:10.5465/amp.2014.0013

Doody, O., & Noonan, M. (2013). Preparing and conducting interviews to collect data. *Nurse Researcher, 20*(5), 28-32. doi:10.7748/nr2013.05.20.5.28.e327

Englander, M. (2012). The interview: data collection in descriptive phenomenological human scientific research. *Journal of Phenomenological Psychology, 43*, 13. doi:10.1163/156916212X632943

Erridge, A., & Hennigan, S. (2012). Sustainable procurement in health and social care in Northern Ireland. *Public Money & Management, 32*(5), 363-370. doi:10.1080/09540962.2012.703422

Etro, F., & Cella, M. (2013). Equilibrium principal-agent contracts: Competition and R&D incentives. *Journal of Economics & Management Strategy, 22,* 488-512. doi:10.1111/jems.12021

Fahed-Sreih, J., & Morin-Delerm, S. (2012). A perspective on leadership in small businesses: Is the need for achievement a motive in predicting success? *International Journal of Entrepreneurship, 16*, 1-23. Retrieved from
http://www.alliedacademies.org/Public/Journals/JournalDetails.aspx?jid=7

Fan, X., & Sun, S. (2014). Generalizability theory as a unifying framework of measurement reliability in adolescent research. *Journal of Early Adolescence, 34*, 38-65. doi:10.1177/0272431613482044

Fayezi, S., O'Loughlin, A., & Zutshi, A. (2012). Agency theory and supply chain management: A structured literature review. *Supply Chain Management: An International Journal, 17*, 556-570. doi:10.1108/13598541211258618

Federal Acquisition Regulation. (2014a). *Contractor performance information.* Retrieved from
http://acquisition.gov/far/current/html/Subpart%2042_15.html

Federal Acquisition Regulation. (2014b). *Definitions.* Retrieved from
http://www.acquisition.gov/Far/current/html/Subpart%202_1.html

Federal Acquisition Regulation. (2014c). *Dissemination of information.* Retrieved from
http://www.acquisition.gov/far/html/Subpart%205_1.html

Federal Acquisition Regulation. (2014d). *Set-asides for small business.* Retrieved from
http://www.acquisition.gov/far/html/Subpart%2019_5.html

Federal Acquisition Regulation. (2014e). *Size Standard.* Retrieved from
https://acquisition.gov/far/current/html/Subpart%2019_1.html

Fernandez, S. (2009). Understanding contracting performance an empirical analysis. *Administration & Society, 41*, 67-100.

doi:10.1177/0095399708330257

Fernandez, S., Malatesta, D., & Smith, C. R. (2013). Race, gender, and government contracting: Different explanations or new prospects for theory? *Public Administration Review, 73,* 109-120. doi:10.1111/j.1540-6210.2012.02684.x

Flynn, A., & Davis, P. (2014). Theory in public procurement research. *Journal of Public Procurement, 14,* 139-180. Retrieved from http://www.ippa.org/pub_journal.html

Gardenal, F. (2013). A model to measure e-procurement impacts on organizational performance. *Journal of Public Procurement, 13,* 215-242. Retrieved from http://www.ippa.org/pub_journal.html

Gauthier, J., & Wooldridge, B. (2012). Influences on sustainable innovation adoption: Evidence from leadership in energy and environmental design. *Business Strategy & the Environment, 21*(2), 98-110. doi:10.1002/bse.716

General Services Administration. (2016). *Frequently Asked Questions: Suspension & Debarment.* Retrieved from http://www.gsa .gov/portal/content/192903

Gianakis, G., & McCue, C. (2012). Supply management concepts in local government: Four case studies. *Journal of Public Procurement, 12,* 109-141. Retrieved from http://pracademics.com/index.php/jopp

Gill, M. J. (2014). The possibilities of phenomenology for organizational research. *Organizational Research Methods, 17,* 118-137. doi:10.1177/1094428113518348

Girth, A. M. (2014). A closer look at contract accountability: Exploring the determinants of sanctions for unsatisfactory contract performance. *Journal of Public Administration Research and Theory, 24,* 317-348. doi:10.1093/jopart/mus033

Giunipero, L. C., Hooker, R. E., & Denslow, D. (2012). Purchasing and supply management sustainability: Drivers and barriers. *Journal of Purchasing and Supply Management, 18,* 258-269. doi:10.1016/j.pursup.2012.06.003

Glock, C. H., & Broens, M. G. (2013). Size and structure in the purchasing function: Evidence from German municipalities. *Journal of Public Procurement, 13,* 1-38. Retrieved from http://www.ippa.org/pub_journal.html

Gordon, J., & Patterson, J. A. (2013). Response to Tracy's under the "big tent" establishing universal criteria for evaluating qualitative research. *Qualitative Inquiry, 19,* 689-695. doi:10.1177/1077800413500934

Gordon, W. (2011). Behavioral economics and qualitative research: A marriage made in heaven? *International Journal of Market Research, 53,* 171-185. doi:10.2501/IJMR-53-2-171-186

Graves, L. M., Sarkis, J., & Zhu, Q. (2013). How transformational leadership and employee motivation combine to predict employee proenvironmental behaviors in China. *Journal of Environmental Psychology, 35,* 81-91. doi:10.1016/j.jenvp.2013.05.002

Grob, S., & Benn, S. (2014). Conceptualising the adoption of sustainable procurement: an institutional theory perspective. *Australasian Journal of Environmental Management, 21,* 11-21. doi:10.1080/14486563.2013.878259

Grudinschi, D., Sintonen, S., & Hallikas, J. (2014). Relationship risk perception and determinants of the collaboration fluency of buyer-supplier relationships in public service procurement. *Journal of Purchasing and Supply Management, 20*(2), 82-91. doi:10.1016/j.pursup.2014.03.004

Gupta, S. (2013). Serving the "bottom of pyramid": A servant leadership perspective. *Journal of Leadership, Accountability & Ethics, 10*(3), 98-106. Retrieved from http://www.na-businesspress.com/jlaeopen.html

Harrison, R. L. (2013). Using mixed methods designs in the Journal of Business Research, 1990–2010. *Journal of Business Research, 66*, 2153-2162. doi:10.1016/j.jbusres.2012.01.006

Heracleous, L., & Lan, L. L. (2012). Agency theory, institutional sensitivity, and inductive reasoning: Towards a legal perspective. *Journal of Management Studies, 49*, 223-239. doi:10.1111/j.1467-6486.2011.01009.x

Hiles, J. (2015). *Federal contracting: 13 steps to increase your CPARS ratings* [PDF Reader Version]. Retrieved from http://www.amazon.com/

Hiles, J., & Wells, W. E. (2015). *Winning with past performance: Strategies for industry and government.* Tysons Corner, VA: Management Concepts Inc.

Holloway, D. E. (2013). *Understanding leadership in small business from the perspectives of practitioners* (Doctoral dissertation). Available from ProQuest Dissertations and Theses database. (UMI No. 3606071)

Houghton, C., Casey, D., Shaw, D., & Murphy, K. (2013). Rigour in qualitative case-study research. *Nurse Researcher, 20*(4), 12-17. doi:10.7748/nr2013.03.20.4.12.e326

Jacob, S. A., & Furgerson, S. P. (2012). Writing interview protocols and conducting interviews: Tips for students new to the field of qualitative research. *Qualitative Report, 17.* Retrieved from http://www.nova.edu/ssss/QR/

Jacobi, O., & Weiss, A. (2013). The effect of time on default remedies for breach of contract. *International Review of Law and Economics, 35*, 13-25. doi:10.1016/j.irle.2012.11.004

Jensen, M. C., & Meckling, W. H. (1976). Theory of the firm: Managerial behavior, agency costs and ownership. *Journal of Financial Economics 3*, 305-360. Retrieved from http://jfe.rochester.edu

Joaquin, M. E., & Greitens, T. J. (2012). Contract management capacity breakdown? An analysis of U.S. local governments. *Public Administration Review, 72*, 807-816. doi:10.1111/j.1540-6210.2012.02587.x

Johnston, J. M., & Girth, A. M. (2012). Government contracts and "managing the market" exploring the costs of strategic management responses to weak vendor competition. *Administration & Society, 44*, 3-29. doi:10.1177/0095399711417396

Kahlke, R. M. (2014). Generic qualitative approaches: Pitfalls and benefits of methodological mixology. *International Journal of Qualitative Methods, 13*, 37-52. Retrieved from http://www.iiqm.ualberta.ca/InternationalJournalofQualitati.aspx

Kai, Q., Wei, C., & Meng-lin, B. (2014). Green supply chain knowledge sharing mechanism based on principal-agent theory. *Journal of*

Chemical & Pharmaceutical Research, 6, 1631-1639. Retrieved from http://jocpr.com/

Kayemuddin, M. D. (2012). Leadership in small business in Bangladesh. *International Journal of Entrepreneurship, 16,* 25-35. Retrieved from http://www.alliedacademies.org/Public/Journals/JournalDetails.aspx?jid=7

Khan, A. Z., & Adnan, N. (2014). Impact of leadership styles on organizational performance. *International Journal of Management Sciences, 2,* 501-515. Retrieved from http://www.rassweb.com/details-ms/

Kiron, D., Kruschwitz, N., Haanaes, K., Reeves, M., & Goh, E. (2013). The innovation bottom line. *MIT Sloan Management Review, 5.* Retrieved from http://sloanreview.mit.edu/reports/sustainability-innovation/

Kisely, S., & Kendall, E. (2011). Critically appraising qualitative research: A guide for clinicians more familiar with quantitative techniques. *Australasian Psychiatry, 19,* 364-367. doi:10.3109/10398562.2011.562508

Korman, P. T. (2014). Balancing the scales: Applying the fair compensation principle to determine recovery for commercial item contracts terminated for the government's convenience. *Military Law Review, 220,* 218-241. Retrieved from https://www.jagcnet.army.mil/DOCLIBS/MILITARYLAWREVIEW.NSF

Lambert V., Lambert, C. (2012). Qualitative descriptive research: An acceptable design. *Pacific Rim International Journal of Nursing Research, 16*(4), 255-256. Retrieved from http://thailand.digitaljournals.org/

Lamothe, M., & Lamothe, S. (2012a). To trust or not to trust? What matters in local government-vendor relationships? *Journal of Public Administration Research and Theory, 22,* 867-892. Retrieved from http://jpart.oxfordjournals.org/

Lamothe, M., & Lamothe, S. (2012b). What determines the formal versus relational nature of local government contracting? *Urban Affairs Review, 48,* 322-353. doi:10.1177/1078087411432418

Lasky, A. (2013). Shedding light on suspensions and debarments. *Contract Management, 53*(2), 16-27. Retrieved from http://www.ncmahq.org

Latham, J. R. (2013a). A framework for leading the transformation to performance excellence part I: CEO perspectives on forces, facilitators, and strategic leadership systems. *Quality Management Journal, 20*(2), 12-33. Retrieved from http://asq.org/pub/qmj/

Latham, J. R. (2013b). A framework for leading the transformation to performance excellence part II: CEO perspectives on leadership behaviors, individual leader characteristics, and organizational culture. *Quality Management Journal, 20*(3), 19-40. Retrieved from http://asq.org/pub/qmj/

Latham, J. R. (2014). Leadership for quality and innovation: Challenges, theories, and a framework for future research. *Quality Management Journal, 21,* 11-15. Retrieved from http://asq.org/pub/qmj/

Lee, J., & Pati, N. (2012). New insights on the operational links between corporate sustainability and firm performance in service industries. *International Journal of Business Insights & Transformation, 4,* 80-93.

Retrieved from http://www.ijbit.org/

Leko, M. M. (2014). The value of qualitative methods in social validity research. *Remedial and Special Education, 35*, 275-286. doi:10.1177/0741932514524002

Lincoln, Y. S., & Guba, E. G. (1985). *Naturalistic inquiry.* Newbury Park, CA: Sage.

Lourenço, I. C., Callen, J. L. Branco, M. C., & Curto, J. D. (2014). The value relevance of reputation for sustainability leadership. *Journal of Business Ethics, 119*, 17-28. doi:10.1007/s10551-012-1617-7

Lu, J. (2013). How political are government contracting decisions? An examination of human service contracting determinants. *Public Administration Quarterly, 37*, 182-207. Retrieved from http://www.spaef.com

Madill, A. (2011). Interaction in the semi-structured interview: A comparative analysis of the use of and response to indirect complaints. *Qualitative Research in Psychology, 8*, 333-353. doi:10.1080/14780880903521633

Makipere, K., & Yip, G. (2008). Sustainable leadership. *Business Strategy Review, 19*, 64-67. doi:10.1111/j.1467-8616.2008.00521.x

Mangioni, V., & McKerchar, M. (2013). Strengthening the validity and reliability of the focus group as a method in tax research. *eJournal of Tax Research, 11*, 176-190. Retrieved from https://www.business.unsw.edu.au/research/publications/atax-journal

Margarian, A. (2014). One bird in the hand ... : the local organization of surveys and qualitative data. *Forum: Qualitative Social Research, 15*(3). Retrieved from http://nbn-resolving.de/urn:nbn:de:0114-fqs1403130

Matsa, D. A., & Amalia R. M. (2011). Chipping away at the glass ceiling: Gender spillovers in corporate leadership. *American Economic Review, 101*, 635-639. doi:10.1257/aer.101.3.635

Matsa, D. A., & Miller, A. R. (2011). Workforce reductions at women-owned businesses in the United States. *Industrial & Labor Relations Review, 67*, 422-452. Retrieved from http://www.ilr.cornell.edu/ilrreview/

McCann, J., & Sweet, M. (2014). The perceptions of ethical and sustainable leadership. *Journal of Business Ethics, 121*, 373-383. doi:10.1007/s10551-013-1704-4

Mcdonald, M. L., & Westphal, J. D. (2013). Access denied: Low mentoring of women and minority first-time directors and its negative effects on appointments to additional boards. *Academy of Management Journal, 56*, 1169-1198. doi:10.5465/amj.2011.0230

McKevitt, D., Davis, P., Woldring, R., Smith, K., Flynn, A., & McEvoy, E. (2012). An exploration of management competencies in public sector procurement. *Journal of Public Procurement, 12*, 333-355. Retrieved from http://www.ippa.org/pub_journal.html

Melissen, F., & Reinders, H. (2012). A reflection on the Dutch Sustainable Public Procurement Programme. *Journal of Integrative Environmental Sciences, 9*, 27-36. doi:10.1080/1943815X.2012.658815

Metcalf, L., & Benn, S. (2012). The corporation is ailing social technology: Creating a 'fit for purpose' design for sustainability. *Journal of Business Ethics, 111*, 195-210. doi:10.1007/s10551-012-1201-1

Metcalf, L., & Benn, S. (2013). Leadership for sustainability: An evolution of leadership ability. *Journal of Business Ethics, 112*, 369-384. doi:10.1007/s10551-012-1278-6

Miemczyk, J., Johnsen, T. E., & Macquet, M. (2012). Sustainable purchasing and supply management: A structured literature review of definitions and measures at the dyad, chain and network levels. *Supply Chain Management, 17*, 478-496. doi:10.1108/13598541211258564

Mirocha, J., Bents, R., LaBrosse, M., & Rietow, K. (2013). Strategies for developing leaders in small to medium sized firms: An analysis of best practices in the most successful firms. *Organization Development Journal, 31*(3), 23-38. Retrieved from http://www.emeraldgrouppublishing.com/lodj.htm

Mittal, R., & Dorfman, P. W. (2012). Servant leadership across cultures. *Journal of World Business, 47*, 555-570. doi:10.1016/j.jwb.2012.01.009

Morse, W. C., Lowery, D. R., & Steury, T. (2014). Exploring saturation of themes and spatial locations in qualitative public participation geographic information systems research. *Society & Natural Resources, 27*, 557-571. doi:10.1080/08941920.2014.888791

Moustakas, C. (1994). *Phenomenological research methods.* Thousand Oaks, CA: Sage.

Newman-Storen, R. (2014). Leadership in sustainability: Creating an interface between creativity and leadership theory in dealing with "Wicked Problems." *Sustainability, 6*, 5955-5967. doi:10.3390/su6095955

Never, B., & de Leon, E. (2014). The effect of government contracting on non-profit human service organizations: Impacts of an evolving relationship. *Human Service Organizations: Management, Leadership & Governance, 38*, 258-270, doi:10.1080/23303131.2014.896300

Perego, P., & Kolk, A. (2012). Multinationals' accountability on sustainability: The evolution of third-party assurance of sustainability reports. *Journal of Business Ethics, 110*, 173-190. doi:10.1007/s10551-012-1420-5

Plane, C. V., & Green. A. N. (2012). Buyer-supplier collaboration: The aim of FM procurement? *Facilities, 30*, 152-163. doi:10.1108/02632771211202851

Polit, D.F. & Hungler, B.P. (2013). *Essentials of nursing research: Methods, appraisal, and utilization* (8th Edition ed.). Philadelphia, PA: Wolters Kluwer/Lippincott Williams and Wilkins.

Preuss, L. (2011). On the contribution of public procurement to entrepreneurship and small business policy. *Entrepreneurship & Regional Development, 23*, 787-814. doi:10.1080/08985626.2010.546433

Protection of Human Subjects, Title 45 C.F.R. pt. 46 (1974).

Prywes, Y. (2011). Organization history (OHx). *OD Practitioner, 43*(2), 40-45. Retrieved from http://www.odnetwork.org/?Publications

Psychogios, A. G., & Garev, S. (2012). Understanding complexity leadership behaviour in SMEs: Lessons from a turbulent business environment. *Emergence: Complexity & Organization, 14*(3), 1-22. Retrieved from http://emergentpublications.com/

Robertson, J. L., & Barling, J. (2013). Greening organizations through leaders' influence on employees' pro-environmental behaviors. *Journal* of *Organizational Behavior, 34,* 176-194. doi:10.1002/job.1820

Robinson, O. C. (2013). Sampling in interview-based qualitative research: A theoretical and practical guide. *Qualitative Research in Psychology, 11,* 25-41. doi:10.1080/14780887.2013.801543

Rodham, K., Fox, F., & Doran, N. (2013). Exploring analytical trustworthiness and the process of reaching consensus in interpretative phenomenological analysis: Lost in transcription. *International Journal of Social Research Methodology, 18,* 59-71. doi:10.1080/13645579.2013.852368

Sanjari, M., Bahramnezhad, F., Khoshnava Fomani, F., Shoghi, M., & Cheraghi, M. (2014). Ethical challenges of researchers in qualitative studies: the necessity to develop a specific guideline. *Journal of Medical Ethics and History of Medicine, 7,* 14. Retrieved from http://jmehm.tums.ac.ir

Schneider, S. K., & George, W. M. (2011). Servant leadership versus transformational leadership in voluntary service organizations. *Leadership & Organization Development Journal, 32,* 60-77. doi:10.1108/01437731111099283

Schou, L., Høstrup, H., Lyngsø, E. E., Larsen, S., & Poulsen, I. (2012). Validation of a new assessment tool for qualitative research articles. *Journal of Advanced Nursing, 68,* 2086-2094. doi:10.1111/j.1365-2648.2011.05898.x

Shields, P., & Rangarjan, N. (2013). *A playbook for research methods: Integrating conceptual frameworks and project management.* Stillwater, OK: New Forums Press.

Shull, F. (2013). A lifetime guarantee. *IEEE Software, 30*(6), 4-8. doi:10.1109/MS.2013.119

Simon, M. K. (2011). Dissertation and scholarly research: Recipes for success (2011 ed.). Seattle, WA, Dissertation Success.

Sinkovics, R., & Alfoldi, E. (2012). Progressive focusing and trustworthiness in qualitative research. *Management International Review (MIR), 52,* 817-845. doi:10.1007/s11575-012-0140-5

Small Business Administration. (2014a). *The small business act.* Retrieved from https://www.sba.gov/sites/default/files/files/Small%20Business%20Act.pdf

Small Business Administration. (2014b). *U.S. Small Business Administration strategic plan fiscal years 2014-2018.* Retrieved from https://www.sba.gov/sites/default/files/aboutsbaarticle/to%20SBA%20%20FY2014-2018%20Strategic%20Plan.pdf

Small Business Administration. (2014c). *What is SBA's definition of a small business concern?* Retrieved from https://www.sba.gov/content/what-sbas-definition-small-business-concern

Small Business Administration. (2015). *Dynamic small business search. Retrieved from* http://dsbs.sba.gov/dsbs/search/dsp_dsbs.cfm

Smith, C. R., & Fernandez, S. (2010). Equity in federal contracting: Examining the link between minority representation and federal procurement decisions. *Public Administration Review, 70,* 87-96. doi:10.1111/j.1540-6210.2009.02113.x

Smith, J., Haniffa, R., & Fairbrass, J. (2011). A conceptual framework for investigating 'capture' in corporate sustainability reporting assurance. *Journal of Business Ethics, 99*, 425-439. doi:10.1007/s10551-010-0661-4

Smith, J. A., Flowers, P., & Larkin, M. (2009). *Interpretative phenomenological analysis: Theory, method and research.* Thousand Oaks, CA: Sage.

Snider, K. F., Kidalov, M. V., & Rendon, R. G. (2013). Diversity governance by convenience? Federal contracting for minority-owned small businesses. *Public Administration Quarterly, 37*, 393-432. Retrieved from http://www.spaef.com

Sotiriadou, P., Brouwers, J., & Le, T. A. (2014). Choosing a qualitative data analysis tool: A comparison of NVivo and Leximancer. *Annals of Leisure Research, 17*, 218-234. doi:10.1080/11745398.2014.902292

Sousa, D. (2014). Phenomenological psychology: Husserl's static and genetic methods. *Journal of Phenomenological Psychology, 45*, 27-60. doi:10.1163/15691624-12341267

Steinle, C., Schiele, H., & Ernst, T. (2014). Information asymmetries as antecedents of opportunism in buyer-supplier relationships: Testing principal-agent theory. *Journal of Business-to-Business Marketing, 21*, 123-140. doi:10.1080/1051712X.2014.903457

Stentz, J. E., Plano Clark, V. L., & Matkin, G. S. (2012). Applying mixed methods to leadership research: A review of current practices. *Leadership Quarterly, 23*, 1173-1183. doi:10.1016/j.leaqua.2012.10.001

Strand, R. (2014). Strategic leadership of corporate sustainability. *Journal of Business Ethics, 123*, 687-706. doi:10.1007/s10551-013-2017-3

Stuart, H. J. (2013). Positioning the corporate brand as sustainable: Leadership de rigueur. *Journal of Brand Management, 20*, 793-799. doi:10.1057/bm.2013.17

Suri, H. (2011). Purposeful sampling in qualitative research synthesis. *Qualitative Research Journal, 11*(2), 63-75. doi:10.3316/QRJ1102063

Tao, G., & Jingjing, W. (2011). A study of the owner's commission model and incentive contract based on principal-agent relationship. *Systems Engineering Procedia, 1*, 399-405. doi:10.1016/j.sepro.2011.08.060

Tate, W. L., Ellram, L. M., & Dooley, K. J. (2012). Environmental purchasing and supplier management (EPSM): Theory and practice. *Journal of Purchasing and Supply Management, 18*, 173-188. doi:10.1016/j.pursup.2012.07.001

Thomas, E., & Magilvy, J. K. (2011). Qualitative rigor or research validity in qualitative research. *Journal for Specialists in Pediatric Nursing, 16*, 151-155. doi:10.1111/j.1744-6155.2011.00283.x

Tideman, S., Arts, M., & Zandee, D. (2013). Sustainable leadership: Towards a workable definition. *Journal of Corporate Citizenship, 49*, 17-33. doi:10.9774/GLEAF.4700.2013.ma.00004

Truong, H.-H. M., Grasso, M., Chen, Y.-H., Kellogg, T. A., Robertson, T., Curotto, A., ... McFarland, W. (2013). Balancing theory and practice in respondent-driven sampling: A case study of innovations developed to overcome recruitment challenges. *PLoS ONE, 8*(8), 1-7. doi:10.1371/journal.pone.0070344

U.S. Census Bureau. (2016). *North American Industry Classification*

System. Retrieved from http://www.census.gov/eos/www/naics/

U.S. General Accounting Office. (1994). *Supply contract terminations: GSA is missing opportunities to recover costs from vendor default* (GGD-94-137). Retrieved from http://www.gao.gov/assets/220/219674.pdf

U.S. Department of Veterans Affairs. (2015). *Vendor information pages.* Retrieved from https://www.vip.vetbiz.gov/

U.S. General Accounting Office. (2013). *Contractor performance: DOD actions to improve the reporting of past performance information* (GAO-13-589). Retrieved from http://www.gao.gov/assets/660/655594.pdf

U.S. General Accounting Office. (2014a). Contractor Performance: Actions taken to improve reporting of past performance information (GAO-14-707). Retrieved from http://www.gao.gov/assets/670/665238.pdf

U.S. General Accounting Office. (2014b). *Strategic sourcing: Selected agencies should develop performance measures on inclusion of small businesses and OMB should improve monitoring* (GAO-14-126). Retrieved from http://www.gao.gov/assets/670/660322.pdf

Vaismoradi, M., Turunen, H., & Bondas, T. (2013). Content analysis and thematic analysis: Implications for conducting a qualitative descriptive study. *Nursing & Health Sciences, 15,* 398-405. doi:10.1111/nhs.12048

Vanclay, F., Baines, J. T., & Taylor, C. N. (2013). Principles for ethical research involving humans: Ethical professional practice in impact assessment, Part I. *Impact Assessment and Project Appraisal, 31,* 243-253. doi:10.1080/14615517.2013.850307

Van Manen, M. (1990). *Researching lived experience: Human science for an action sensitive pedagogy.* New York: SUNY Press.

Van Slyke, D. M. (2007). Agents or stewards: Using theory to understand the government-non-profit social service contracting relationship. *Journal of Public Administration Research and Theory, 17,* 157-187. doi:10.1093/jopart/mul012

Venkatesh, V., Brown, S. A., & Bala, H. (2013). Bridging the qualitative-quantitative divide: Guidelines for conducting mixed methods research in information systems. *Management Information Systems Quarterly, 37,* 21-54. Retrieved from http://www.misq.org/

Walker, H., Miemczyk, J., Johnsen, T., & Spencer, R. (2012). Sustainable procurement: Past, present and future. *Journal of Purchasing and Supply Management, 18,* 201-206. doi:10.1016/j.pursup.2012.11.003

Walker, J. L. (2012). The use of saturation in qualitative research. *Canadian Journal of Cardiovascular Nursing, 22,* Institutional Review Board, 37-41. Retrieved from http://pappin.com/journals/cjcn.php

White, D. E., Oelke, N. D., & Friesen, S. (2012). Management of a large qualitative data set: Establishing trustworthiness of the data. *International Journal of Qualitative Methods, 11,* 244-258. Retrieved from http://ejournals.library.ualberta.ca/index.php/IJQM/

Wiseman, R. M., Cuevas-Rodriguez, G. and Gomez-Mejia, L. R. (2012). Towards a social theory of agency. *Journal of Management Studies, 49,* 202-222. doi:10.1111/j.1467-6486.2011.01016.x

Witesman, E. M., & Fernandez, S. (2013). Government contracts with private organizations are there differences between non-profits and for-profits? *Non-profit and Voluntary Sector Quarterly, 42,* 689-715. doi:10.1177/0899764012442592

Witko, C. (2011). Campaign contributions, access, and government contracting. *Journal of Public Administration Research and Theory, 21,* 761-778. Retrieved from http://jpart.oxfordjournals.org/

Yan, L., & Yan, J. (2013). Leadership, organizational citizenship behavior, and innovation in small business: An empirical study. *Journal of Small Business and Entrepreneurship, 26,* 183-199. doi:10.1080/08276331.2013.771863

Yang, Y. N., Kumaraswamy, M. M., Pam, H. J., & Mahesh, G. (2010). Integrated qualitative and quantitative methodology to assess validity and credibility of models for bridge maintenance management system development. *Journal of Management in Engineering, 27,* 149-158. doi:10.1061/(ASCE)ME.1943-5479.0000051

Yin, R. K. (2009). *Case study research: Design and methods* (4th ed.). Thousand Oaks, CA: Sage.

APPENDICES

APPENDIX A

Appendix A: Invitation to Participate

Dear 'Name',

My name is Tamara Williams and I am currently a doctoral student at Walden University. I am investigating strategies small business leaders use to obtain positive performance ratings in government contracting by understanding at least 20 small business leader's experiences. I would greatly appreciate your participation.

This would involve completing a demographic questionnaire, which will take about 10 minutes and participate in an interview, which would take about 45 minutes in a private meeting room at the location of your choosing most convenient for you. Interviews will be conducted at a time that is convenient for you.

The information from the demographic questionnaire and interviews will be kept strictly confidential and no one who participates will be identified in any of the study's report that I prepare.

If you have any questions about the study, please feel free to email me at xxxxxx.xxxxxxxxx@waldenu.edu or give me a call at (xxx) xxx-xxxx.

If you are interested in participating in the study and/or would like to recommend another small business leader located within 30 miles of Washington, DC, with a favorable performance rating on at least three government contracting opportunity to be a participant in this study, please complete the questions below in a reply email to me.

Thank you in advance for your consideration and assistance with my research project.

Sincerely,
Tamara Williams

If you are interested in participating in the study, please complete the questions below in a reply email to me at xxxx @waldenu.edu:

1. What is your name?

2. What is your company's socio-economic status?
   (Please select by bolding your answer)
   a. Small Business
   b. 8(a)
   c. Women-Owned
   d. Veteran Owned Small Business
   e. Service-Disabled, Veteran-Owned, Small
      Business
   f. HUB-Zone Small Business
   g. Alaskan Native
   h. Other _____

3. What is your contact information?

APPENDIX B

Appendix B: National Institutes of Health Certificate

Certificate of Completion

The National Institutes of Health (NIH) Office of Extramural Research certifies that **Tamara Williams** successfully completed the NIH Web-based training course "Protecting Human Research Participants".

Date of completion: 06/29/2014

Certification Number: 1496157

APPENDIX C

Appendix C: Classification Questionnaire
Directions: Please answer the following classification questions:

1. Are you registered in FedBizzOps?

2. Are you registered in System for Award Management?

3. How many CPARS ratings has your company received?
   a. 0
   b. 1-5
   c. 5-10
   d. More than 10

4. What NAICS code have you used when providing supplies/services to the Government?

5. Select the socio-economic category of your company (you may select more than one)
   a. Small Business
   b. 8a
   c. Women-Owned
   d. Veteran Owned Small Business
   e. Service Disabled Veteran Owned Small

Business
f. HUB Zone Small business
g. Alaskan Native
h. Other _____

6. How would you define success?

APPENDIX D

Appendix D: Interview Guide

Introduction

- Welcome participant and introduce myself.
- Explain the general purpose of the interview and why the participant was chosen.
- Discuss the purpose and process of interview.
- Explain the presence and purpose of the recording equipment.
- Outline general ground rules and interview guidelines such as being prepared for the interviewer to interrupt to assure that all the topics can be covered.
- Review break schedule and where the restrooms are located.
- Address the assurance of confidentiality.
- Inform the participant that information discussed is going to be analyzed as a whole and participant's name will not be used in any analysis of the interview.

Discussion Purpose

The purpose of this qualitative descriptive research study is to bridge gaps in information by exploring strategies some small business leaders use to achieve positive performance ratings in government contracting by interviewing at least 20 small business leaders located within 30 miles of Washington, DC, with a favorable performance rating on at least three government contracting opportunity.

Discussion Guidelines

Interviewer will explain:

Please respond directly to the questions and if you don't understand the question, please let me know. I am here to ask questions, listen, and answer any questions you might have. If we seem to get stuck on a topic, I may interrupt you. I will keep your identity, participation, and remarks private. Please speak openly and honestly. This session will be tape recorded because I do not want to miss any comments.

General Instructions

When responding to questions that will be asked of you in the interview, please exclude all identifying information, such as your name and names of other parties. Your identity will be kept confidential and any information that will permit identification will be removed from the analysis.

Interview Questions

Q1: What leadership strategies do you find most effective for achieving positive performance ratings in government contracts?

Q2: What leadership behaviors do leaders/managers employ that are attributes to positive performance ratings in government contracts?

Q3: How do these attributes influence contract performance ratings?

Q4: How does the contractor–government relationship impede or affect performance ratings?

Q5: What are the impediments or obstacles that small business leaders face when performing in government contracts?

Q6: What resources do business leaders use to assist in achieving positive performance ratings in government contracts?

Q7: What restrictions, if any, discourage small business representatives from achieving positive performance ratings in government contracting opportunities?

Q8: What additional information can you provide to improve leadership effectiveness in small businesses' contracting performance?

Q9: What programs and information will help leaders of small businesses seeking to improve performance ratings in government contracts?

Q10: What programs or information do you suggest to leaders of small businesses seeking to obtain government-contracting opportunities?

Conclusion

- Discuss the transcription review process with participant, ask and answer any questions, and thank the participant for his or her time.

APPENDIX E

Appendix E: IRB Approval

Dear Ms. Williams,

This email is to notify you that the Institutional Review Board (IRB) has approved your application for the study entitled, "Small Business Leaders Perceptions of Factors Facilitating Successful Performance in Government Contracts."

Your approval # is 05-12-15-0481984. You will need to reference this number in your dissertation and in any future funding or publication submissions. Also attached to this e-mail is the IRB approved consent form. Please note, if this is already in an on-line format, you will need to update that consent document to include the IRB approval number and expiration date.

Your IRB approval expires on May 11, 2016. One month before this expiration date, you will be sent a Continuing Review Form, which must be submitted if you wish to collect data beyond the approval expiration date.

Your IRB approval is contingent upon your adherence to the exact procedures described in the final version of the IRB application document that has been submitted as of this date. This includes maintaining your current status with the university. Your IRB approval is only valid while you are an actively enrolled student at Walden University. If you need to take a leave of absence or are otherwise unable to remain actively enrolled, your IRB approval is suspended. Absolutely NO participant recruitment or data collection may occur while a student is not actively enrolled.

If you need to make any changes to your research staff or procedures, you must obtain IRB approval by submitting the IRB Request for Change in Procedures Form. You will receive confirmation with a status update of the request within 1 week of submitting the change request form and are not permitted to implement changes prior to receiving approval. Please note that Walden University does not accept responsibility or liability for research activities conducted without the IRB's approval, and the University will not accept or grant credit for student work that fails to comply with the policies and procedures related to ethical standards in research.

When you submitted your IRB application, you made a commitment to communicate both discrete adverse events and general problems to the IRB within 1 week of their occurrence/realization. Failure to do so may result in invalidation of data, loss of academic credit, and/or loss of legal protections otherwise available to the researcher.

Both the Adverse Event Reporting form and Request for Change in Procedures form can be obtained at the IRB

section of the Walden website:
http://academicguides.waldenu.edu/researchcenter/orec

Researchers are expected to keep detailed records of their research activities (i.e., participant log sheets, completed consent forms, etc.) for the same period of time they retain the original data. If, in the future, you require copies of the originally submitted IRB materials, you may request them from Institutional Review Board.

Sincerely,

Libby Munson
Research Ethics Support Specialist
Office of Research Ethics and Compliance

Office address for Walden University:
100 Washington Avenue South, Suite 900
Minneapolis, MN 55401
Information about the Walden University Institutional Review Board, including instructions for application, may be found at this link:
http://academicguides.waldenu.edu/researchcenter/orec

INDEX

CURRICULUM VITAE

Dr. TAMARA P. WILLIAMS
Washington, DC

EXECUTIVE STATEMENT: EXECUTIVE STATEMENT

Instructor, author, researcher, and Subject Matter Expert (SME) in contracting. As a business owner, Dr. Williams is a strategic specialist in the federal marketplace. She consults on an array of projects such as customer engage, helping companies enter new federal markets, competitive/industry analysis, and organizational develop activities such as helping organizations stand up procurement divisions.

EXPERIENCE PORTFOLIO

Principal Consultant, President and CEO
Aramat & Associates, Inc., Washington, DC
01/16 - present

*   Helps organizations improve their contracting activities by identifying costly procurement processes and offering solutions in implementing Innovative Procurement Practices. We service: 1) Federal State and Local Governments and 2) Government Contractors and Commercial Clients

Senior Contract Specialist
Department of Housing and Urban Development, Washington, DC
11/14 - 12/15

- Lead contracts negotiations and fact-finding sessions, pre-proposal conferences, debriefings.
- Served as Senior Contract Specialist with full authority for directing planning and execution of contractual actions and phases for assigned program clients and programs.
- Obligate millions of dollars annually in support of assigned programs.
- Plan, evaluate, and direct a cost-effective program encompassing extremely large, difficult, and diverse projects.

Supervisory Contract Specialist (Branch Chief)
Department of Veterans Affairs, Washington, DC
12/2012 to 11/2014

- Served as business adviser to VISN personnel for acquisition matters.
- Scheduled, directed, and managed myriad acquisition services to the VISN.
- Managed acquisition operations that supported multiple major medical centers and Community-Based Outpatient Clinics.
- Coordinated and implemented acquisition and financial policies and procedures and provided senior management with expert advice on procurement and financial assistance matters.
- Procured supplies and services using the FAR, VA Acquisition Regulations, public laws, and agency policy.
- Conducted pre-award through contract award by performing market research, reviewing specifications and

SOWs, as well as approving acquisition milestone plans.

Supervisory Procurement Analyst
Department of Health and Human Services
National Institutes of Health, Washington, DC
07/2011 to 12/2012

- Served as Supervisory Team Manager and Contracting Officer for the Department of Health and Human Services (HHS), National Institutes of Health (NIH).
- Managed the team's workload and effort and ensured assignments were accomplished in timely, competent manner.
- Conducted or oversaw the cradle-to-grave procurement of supplies and services using procedures in the FAR, HHS Acquisition Regulations, Public Laws, and Agency policies.
- Provided technical and administrative supervision necessary for accomplishing the work of the team.
- Monitored work to include training staff to perform duties from receipt of procurement requests through contract closeout in Records and Information Management System (RIMS) contracting system.

Contract Specialist
Department of Health and Human Services
Food and Drug Administration, Washington, DC
08/06 - 07/11

- Supported business activities and acquisition for the Food and Drug Administration (FDA). Served as the Contracting Officer in cradle-to-grave contracting, awarding, and administering various contracts ranging to $34M in value
- Assisted contracting officers with complex contract actions in general consulting services, renovations and building

services, construction, A+E services, Information Technology (IT) software/hardware, and systems development.
- Received program requirements, assisted with procurement plans, and determined method of solicitation and type of contract.
- Prepared solicitation to prospective contractors.
- Accepted evaluations bids/proposals/quotations.
- Performed full range of contract administration responsibilities, including issuing modifications.
- Performed administrative duties supporting the contracting function.

Contract Specialist (Government Contractor)
Progressive Technology Federal Systems, Inc.
Washington, DC
01/06 - 08/06

- Performed pre-award, award, and post-award functions with contract specialists on Library of Congress staff.
- Reviewed requisitions to confirm validity.
- Prepared acquisition plans and other solicitation documents in accordance with FAR and Library of Congress policies.
- Used FedBizOpps, to publicly advertise Library's requirements
- Conducted pre-bid/proposal conferences; amended solicitation.
- Evaluated responses received from vendors.
- Performed cost/price analysis; developed pre-negotiation objectives and price negotiation memoranda to obtain and document a fair and reasonable price.
- Conducted and documented a responsibility determination for the proposed contractor.

TEACHING AND TRAINING EXPERIENCE

ADJUNCT PROFESSOR, MBA
Champlain College. VT
03/16 - present

- Taught Project Management courses using the Canvas LMS. Create and maintain course materials in compliance with College and regulatory requirements.
- Assess student learning, provide feedback and support

Dissertation Coach / Proposal Consultant
Aramat & Associates Inc.
01/16 - present

- Coach doctoral students through the dissertation process through training and strategy.
- Assist student select and refine dissertation topics, methodology, and articulate data collection procedures.
- Provide feedback on dissertation drafts and assistance in interpreting and addressing committee feedback to shorten time spent in the review phase.
- Teach goal setting and effective writing practices, to meet objectives.

Adjunct Faculty, Human Resources
Rasmussen College, MN
07/15 - present

- Content expert, instructor and mentor responsible for facilitating Human Resource Information Systems, Introduction to Human Resources Management, Performance-based Training and Instructional Design, and Organizational Behavior Analysis content in a highly effective and engaging learning environment to meet the diverse needs of learners. Conducts live lectures weekly.

- Participate in community service and college in-service training programs and meetings. Participate in professional organizations and professional development activities including webinars, seminars and conferences in various business related subjects.
- Develop, review and adhere to academic policies and procedures for the college.
- Actively participate in advisory boards, student organizations and system committees. Create, implement and evaluate annual professional development plan.

FORMAL DEGREES / EDUCATION

- 2016, Doctor of Business Administration (DBA), Leadership, Walden University
- 2013, Master of Arts, Procurement and Acquisitions Management, Webster University
- 2005, Master of Science, Management. Troy University
- 2001, Bachelor of Science, Health and Fitness, Central Michigan University

PROFESSIONAL TRAINING / CERTIFICATIONS

- 2016 - present, Graduate Certificate, IS/IT Project Management, Villanova University, (Expected conveyance: 3/17)
- 2014, Graduate Certificate, Government Contracting, Webster University
- 2015, Federal Acquisition Certification-Contracting Officer Representative (FAC-COR) Level III
- 2011, Federal Acquisition Certification-Contracting (FAC-C) Level III

PROFESSIONAL PUBLICATIONS

Williams, T. P. (2016). *Strategies For Positive Performance in Government Contracts.* Va. Beach, VA: DBC Publishing.

Williams, T. P. (2015). Sustainability in Government Contracts: A Measure of Performance from the Contractor Perspective. *Mustang Journal of Business and Ethics, 8,* 41–57.

Williams, T. P. (2015). *Small Business Leaders' Perceptions of Strategies Facilitating Positive Performance in Government Contracts* (Doctoral Dissertation). Available from ProQuest Dissertations and Theses database. (UMI No. 3738092)

CONFERENCES PRESENTATIONS

- **10/16, 4th Annual Black Doctoral Network Conference**, **Atlanta, GA.** Presentation of research, "Small Business Leaders Perceptions of Factors Facilitating Successful Performance in Government Contracts."

- **08/15, ICIRS Summer 2015 Conference**, Washington, DC, Presentation of research, "Small Business Leaders Perceptions of Factors Facilitating Successful Performance in Government Contracts."

- **07/15, Walden University Research Symposium**, Washington, DC, Poster Presentation of "Small Business Leaders Perceptions of Factors Facilitating Successful Performance in Government Contracts."

MILITARY EXPERIENCE

United States Air Force
03/02 - 03/06

AWARDS / RECOGNITION

- Air Force Good Conduct Medal
- Air Force Training Ribbon
- Global War on Terrorism Service Medal
- National Defense Service Medal

ABOUT THE AUTHOR

Dr. Tamara P. Williams is a business entrepreneur in the government contracting field and a veteran of the US Air Force. She holds a doctorate in Business Administration, specializing in Leadership. She is the founder of Aramat & Associates, Inc. She serves as an MBA Professor and a HR Professor at online colleges and universities.

Dr. Williams spent 10 years as a Contracting Officer at various federal agencies, before starting Aramat & Associates, Inc. She obtained Masters' degrees in Human Resource Management and Procurement and Acquisitions Management from Troy and Webster Universities. She earned her Doctorate in Business Leadership from Walden University (2016) and holds certifications in Government Contracting, Project Management, and Information Technology.

Dr. Williams conducts research in Business, Leadership, and Federal Acquisitions and has published articles on various aspects of Government Contracting. Her strategic goals for her company, Aramat & Associates, Inc., is to provide experienced consulting services to government contracting entrepreneurs, delivering innovative business research, mission focused solutions, and customer support.

ABOUT THE BOOK

No matter how good the products being delivered to the government customer, performance ratings mostly depend on the relationship. If you are in the first few years of doing business with the government you have probably learned this the hard way. Government Contract work is about networking, mentoring, liaising within the government agency, interacting with agency representatives (customers), and establishing long-term relationships. Those outside government contracting often advise business entrepreneurs in the government contracting field how to compete and how to write proposals, but not many can provide direct training on how to establish and cultivate relationships with government decision makers.

When entrepreneurs enter the government contracting market and struggle to learn the unwritten processes, gaining new contract work feels laborious. This book's content points business developers in the right direction to impress the new or current government agency customers and avoid serious relationship issues. Reading this book will save years of time and money associated with networking in the government contracting industry. It takes years to find resources and access to business owners – or spend a few hours learning critical insight in this book. Readers will receive tips and insight from President's and CEO's of established and active government contracting companies and from Government Contracting Officers' perspectives.

The content contains insight from business owners who are currently in government contracting is a must read book to gain insight for those entering the government contracting arena.

www.ingramcontent.com/pod-product-compliance
Lightning Source LLC
Chambersburg PA
CBHW071630200326
41519CB00012BA/2238